Stress
&
Burnout

FIRST
AID
FOR

T0346531

Elke Van Hoof

Stress & Burnout

FIRST
AID
FOR

LANNOO

Neither the author nor the publisher intend for this book to provide professional advice or services to individual readers. The ideas, processes and suggestions in this book are not intended as a substitute for consultation with a physician or other professional counsellor. All health matters require medical supervision. Neither the author nor the publisher can be held liable for any loss or damage arising from the information or suggestions in this book.

Contents

'The best way to predict the future is to create it.'

— Peter Drucker

Preface

Another book about stress? Hasn't everything already been said about stress? Apparently not. Despite all the (good) literature available on this subject, I still felt the need to write a book with practical tips to better cope with stress. In my opinion, most of the literature limits its focus to a negative approach to stress. I would like to offer a counterweight to this.

The scientific knowledge behind the positive effects of stress has been fascinating me for years. I believe in challenging your status quo and stepping out of your comfort zone in order to achieve a better version of yourself.

I see people as caterpillars who turn into beautiful butterflies every time they reach another milestone.

This book starts from the assumption that stress in itself is not a problem. Indeed, stress is good and even necessary. We all need a healthy amount of stress in our lives, otherwise we would not achieve anything. In this book I will therefore teach you how the stress we inevitably have to deal with can be turned into something positive. But let's not overdramatize things. There is no need to make an appointment with burn-out therapist if you have a tight deadline on a work project or if you are stuck in traffic and the day-care is about to close for the day.

Of course, I do not deny that there are toxic effects connected to stress, especially in the case of chronic stress. As with everything in life, there are limits. Prolonged exposure to (intense) stress does in fact make people ill. And the worst part is that most of us don't even see it coming.

That's why this book is primarily aimed at people whose alarm signals have already started going off. How do you recognize the signals in a timely manner? Are you still in the phase where you have a handle on things or have you already entered the toxic stage? And, most importantly, what can you do about it? Many people are still in the 'pre-clinical' phase. This means they can do something about it themselves. This book is intended as a guide to help them out of the swamp. But even if you're already experiencing burn-out, this book can help provide some insight into what's happening and why it is happening. Before we continue, let me reassure you: it is not your fault. If you have burn-out, share this book with the team who is helping you.

The key to success is to recognize stress as an alarm signal that teaches you to reflect on what is going wrong and what you might do about it. Easy? Absolutely not. Feasible? Definitely! However, my focus is not on analysing problems, but instead the potential that lies within each of us. Even if you have too much negative stress or are burnt-out, there is always something that will still work. Don't become fixated on your problems or shortcomings. Instead, invest your energy in those things that will maximize your potential. Because if you nurture something, it will grow.

Of course, reality is more complicated than that. Stress is always a consequence of a complex interaction between an individual and his or her environment. Simply put, stressful situations can make us ill, but some people are more sensitive to burn-out than others, perhaps, for example, because they are prone to maladaptive perfectionism.

Unfortunately, all too often we still refer to burn-out in black-and-white terms. Often work is singled out as the big culprit. Without a doubt, stress at work does contribute to burn-out, but there are many other factors. If you are dealing with a negative work environment, it's very important to address this. I would therefore also like to use this book to discuss stress at work. Starting the conversation in an inviting, non-confrontational manner is a shared responsibility of both employers *and* employees.

Before you read on, I would like to warn you though. Merely reading this book will not be enough to increase your resilience. It is also important to roll up your sleeves and get to work. No cyclist has ever won a race by sitting on the side lines and cheering. You must put in the work, even if it requires

8

lots of trial and error. Only if you are willing to do that will you be able to maximize your potential. The tests, tips and exercises in this book will help you on your way. They have not just been randomly chosen; they have a scientifically proven effect. I use them in my practice every day. Many of these exercises are action-oriented. People often indicate that they are surprised by the amount of assignments I give them. I know that psychologists are expected to give their clients insight into their behaviours, feelings and reactions. However, neurological research shows that very few psychological problems, including stress, result a lack of such insight. That's why I want to give you a different perspective. If the stress continues, even the deepest insights will not help. Understanding *why* you feel a certain way does not necessarily change *how* you feel.

I often notice that people want to eliminate their stress through counselling, coaching or treatment, but with more than fifteen years of experience I openly wonder whether integrating stress into your life may be better. In my opinion it makes no sense to make yourself less sensitive to stress or to eliminate stress (if that were even a possibility). The question should be: how can you give stress a place in your life?

The main pitfall is that you don't feel you have time to deal with it 'right now'. But you should know that making promises to get started on it tomorrow will likely lead nowhere. Take on this challenge with me. *Make the time*. Even if it's just a few minutes a day, slowly but surely you will notice progress.

Good luck learning to live with your stress!
Elke Van Hoof

1/ Stress: so what?

Check any newspaper and look for the word 'stress'. Chances are you won't have to search very long. In 2016, the online newspaper and magazine archive Gopress had no fewer than 23,459 articles mentioning the word 'stress'. That's more than sixty a day!

Stress is omnipresent. And the tone used by the media, and ourselves, is usually very negative. People have the feeling that they are no longer in control of their lives, that they are chasing after themselves, that they can't handle the pressure (often self-imposed). The term 'stress' has become some type of collective name for everything that goes wrong in our lives, at work, and in society. Stress should therefore be avoided, we think of it as something bad. But should we?

Indeed, scientific research shows that being exposed to excess stress for too long can have adverse health effects. This includes headaches, muscle pain, abdominal pain, stomach issues, problems concentrating, inability to find solutions for seemingly easy problems, irritation, and even aggressive behaviours.

However, I would also like to underline the positive aspects of stress. Stress is the motor that propels us in our lives, the sounding board that tells us (consciously or subconsciously) that action is needed. Without stress, there would be:

- no innovation
- no progress
- no introspection
- no self-development

If you look at stress from this positive point of view, it is an opportunity to learn more about yourself and what you hold dear. After all, stress only appears when something happens that you care about, when something happens that will affect you. Stress and meaning are inextricably connected: you don't get stressed about things you don't care about, and, if you never experience stress, you cannot build a meaningful life.

The solution for anyone suffering from stress therefore does not lie in creating a completely stress-free life. In fact, this will literally drive you insane. Research shows, for example, that subjects isolated in a stimulus-free environment spontaneously begin to hallucinate due to a lack of stress.

'The solution for anyone suffering from stress does therefore not lie in creating a completely stress-free life.'

EXERCISE
Welcoming stress

Step 1/ Recognize when you are experiencing stresss

Allow yourself to acknowledge stress and how it affects your body. You can use the new Apgar score for this exercise (see p. 33), but actually any moment you feel anxious and un-comfortable can be considered for this purpose.

Step 2/ Welcome stress by recognizing it as a response to something you care about

Are you able to establish a connection with what is dear to you? Who or what is at stake and why does it matter to you? Imagine having a conversation with a colleague, but she does not seem to understand what you are trying to tell her. You feel anxious and irritated. You have learned to react by defending yourself because you are experiencing an unpleasant feeling with the conversation. You want to convey the message in a clear way and it doesn't seem to be working. You might ask yourself: "Is she even listen-ing to me?", but this just makes you even more irritated. This usually leads an escalation of the situation.

You could handle it differently though. If you feel anxious and get irritated during a conversation, take a moment to find out why. What is making you feel this way? What is at stake here? As soon as you have figured that out, you can follow it up in the conversation.

It's difficult to do this exercise immediately during a real conversa-tion. So it's better to first think about all the unpleasant conversations you may have had recently and assess what was at stake. (Take a look at the emotions data sheet on p. 16 to help develop a clear picture.) In my case, I have noticed that I can be apprehen-sive of rejection. So if someone bom-bards me with questions without some sort of feedback (showing that they are actively listening and thinking with me), I get annoyed faster than usual. So instead of becoming defensive (which still happens from time to time), I could realize I need room to share my (new) ideas.

Step 3/ Use the energy released by stress instead of wasting your energy trying to control the stress

What can you do in this moment to make things better for yourself and safeguard whatever is at stake for you? To come back to the example above, I could be more proactive and indicate to the person I'm speaking with that I want space to express my idea, instead of going straight into defensive mode. I could also indicate that the barrage of questions makes me feel like there is no room for my (new) ideas. Or I could also say that I appreciate the other person's being 'the devil's advocate', but also that I would like to submit my idea as a whole first before moving to a critique of it. This also gives my conversation partner the opportunity to adjust.

and explain why they feel the need to give me a hard time.

Ideally, you should use sentences like these:
- ▼ **I find that** (*your questions make me anxious*).
- ▼ **I appreciate your** (*critical approach*).
- ▼ **However, I first need to** (*be able to submit the whole idea before hearing a critique*).
- ▼ **How is it in your case?**

What is stress?

We all have to deal with stress. No one escapes it. But what exactly is stress? There are many ways of looking at the phenomenon of stress. I prefer putting the emphasis on the interaction between what is happening to you and how you handle it. **Stress is an alarm signal indicating you should take action.** Such a stress response has roughly three functions:

- detecting danger;
- reducing discomfort to be able to operate as efficiently as possible;
- processing information by detecting differences.

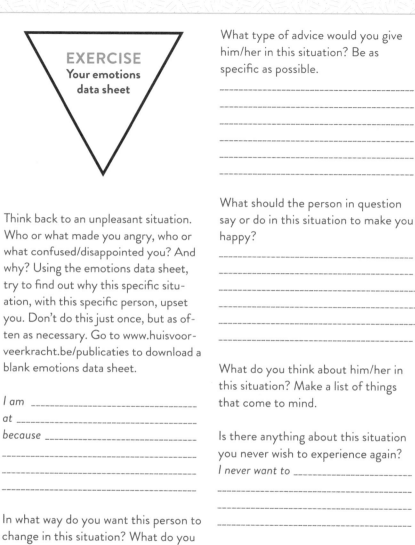

◢ **EXERCISE**
Your emotions data sheet

Think back to an unpleasant situation. Who or what made you angry, who or what confused/disappointed you? And why? Using the emotions data sheet, try to find out why this specific situation, with this specific person, upset you. Don't do this just once, but as often as necessary. Go to www.huisvoorveerkracht.be/publicaties to download a blank emotions data sheet.

I am _____

at _____

because _____

_____

_____

_____

In what way do you want this person to change in this situation? What do you want him/her to do?

I want _____

_____

_____

What type of advice would you give him/her in this situation? Be as specific as possible.

_____

_____

_____

_____

_____

_____

What should the person in question say or do in this situation to make you happy?

_____

_____

_____

_____

_____

_____

What do you think about him/her in this situation? Make a list of things that come to mind.

Is there anything about this situation you never wish to experience again?

I never want to _____

_____

_____

_____

This emotions data sheet provides an insight into what's at stake for you. This book will also show you how to discuss this.

Stress helps you detect danger

First and foremost, stress is a healthy warning signal. Think back to the last time you felt uncomfortable somewhere, for example in a dark street. At a subconscious level, you were screening the situation and your brain told you something was off. Something in your environment was different. That anxious feeling puts you on lookout for danger. This strategy is a part of our instinct to survive. Our behaviour is largely determined by it, even if very often we are not aware of it.

Stress helps you reduce your discomfort to be as efficient as possible

When we experience stress, it is important to spend the available energy wisely. That's why our body will automatically choose the most energy-efficient options. People who experience stress will therefore often choose to eat sugar or fat, for example, because their bodies are telling them that there is an energy shortage. These fast sugars are a good solution in the short term, but in the long term they make us sluggish and overweight. Whether sugar or fat or any other solution is good in the long term is a different question. Our stress response does not engage in long-term thinking.

Stress helps you with processing information by detecting differences

How do we learn something new? By examining how a new fact fits in with what we already know and identifying differences from what we already know. It is not without reason that we teach students to create outlines to create a structure while studying. This is a neat and tidy way to organise and store what we learn. Our stress response helps us here too.

Stress response has a function, even during very traumatic events. It raises enough physical tension (scientists refer to this as *arousal*) to ensure that the situation *and* the elements from that situation are engraved in our memory. This ensures that our stress response will be activated should we ever encounter a situation similar to that earlier experience of trauma. After all, we want to avoid a similar situation in the future. But if we let it go too far, this can cause serious restrictions on our day-to-day functioning. In that case it is important to decrease the power we give to the lessons learned from our traumas so that they do not make us their prisoners.

Take a look at babies and toddlers, for example, and how they throw tantrums when something doesn't go their way. They want to make progress (learn how to grab onto something, learn how to stand, walk, etc.), but are still missing certain skills to reach their goal. They take out their frustration by throwing a tantrum. But once they figure out how to meet that goal, you will see a big smile on their faces, reflecting the satisfaction of victory. After trying to get up for the hundredth time, they have finally done it, firmly standing on both feet. Thanks to their stress response, they have learned something new with each attempt. What helps? What doesn't help? That is how they achieve their new milestone in a relatively efficient way and acquire the new skill.

Healthy stress therefore has a kind of **compass function**. When the alarm sounds, it's time to learn something. Dare to trust your stress compass: it will point out the gaps in your knowledge and skills. Note that this only applies to healthy stress. Toxic stress will make your compass go haywire and it will start pointing in all directions, leading to panic attacks and anxiety, seemingly without any logical reason.

Using stress as a healthy warning signal means reflecting on what has gone well, what could have gone better, and how to deal with it. The following exercise can help you with this.

EXERCISE
Reflecting
on stress

Step 1/ Write down what comes to mind

Look back on your day (or a recent situation). Let your thoughts flow spontaneously. When pleasant thoughts or observations come to mind, write them down (just a few words) under the column 'What went well?'. Write unpleasant thoughts in the column 'What did not go so well?'. This could be anything.

What went well?	What did not go so well?

What do you learn from these two columns?

What will you do differently in the future?

Step 2/ **Look for the lesson**

Wait until no new thoughts/moments come to mind. Take a look at both columns and figure out which lesson you could learn from this. In other words: what do these two lists tell you? This could be a future intention, something from the past that you still need to make up for or just the insight that your day, in spite of everything, still went reasonably well.

Step 3/ **Describe the action**

Translate the lesson into concrete action. Determine what, when and how you will handle it. Determine a time and write it down. Merely reflecting on it is not enough. By writing down the action, the lesson is set and you put yourself in action mode. And connecting stress to action will drop your stress level.

This exercise provides greater clarity about what is going on around you. If you follow these steps it will create a sense of completion, the feeling that you gave it your best shot, and will be able to try it again next time.

The power of our brain

Unlike the heart or lungs, the brain is not a rigid organ that remains unchanged throughout life. The brain is flexible, it can be moulded. The events in your life shape your brain into a unique and individual structure. On the one hand, your brain coordinates what your body needs to do day in and day out, but it also works in the opposite direction: your behaviour can also influence your brain. By always doing the same thing, it becomes automatic, like driving a car with a manual transmission, for example. It's almost impossible not to stall the car the first time you try to drive stick. However, an experienced driver doesn't think twice about what to do put the car into gear. The action has become automatic. The circuit of the brain that helps us drive a car has become through repetition a well-trodden path along which our brain signals follow easily.

Earlier we saw that stress gives you the opportunity to learn something new. Learning is actually nothing else than creating new connections in your brain. Therefore **stress contributes to the plasticity of your brain.** In other words: stress contributes to a vibrant, strong brain. And the better you are able to draw lessons from your stress, the more resilient your brain. But this is only the case if the stress is not crippling you. If you suffer from the negative effects of stress, with only the high-danger alert mode active, it's important to address those symptoms first or to allow sufficient recovery time before starting the learning process.

TIP / BEHAVE LIKE A SMOKER

Take smokers, for example. The only benefit to their (otherwise completely unhealthy) habit is that their addiction requires them to take a break on a regular basis. I'm not saying you should take up smoking, but the unbridled desire for a cigarette can remind you that your brain might need some fresh air as well.

Take regular 5-minute breaks without new stimuli or information
(this does NOT mean surfing the internet or social media) and give your
brain the chance to unwind. You determine for yourself how often you
need such a break. Ideally you should give your brain a 5-minute break
every 45 minutes. Some people are very disciplined and will even set an
alarm to ensure this. Those are usually the people who are very strict and
to the point during meetings, but who happily chat away by the coffee
machine during breaks.

The science of stress is complex, and there is no doubt that chronic stress is toxic. But stress also has clear positive effects. For example, research shows that stressful experiences can have a protective function as well. Alan Schatzberg, connected to prestigious Stanford University, did research into the effect of stress on young humans and squirrel monkeys. In one of their studies, one of his colleagues, Karen Parker, would separate young monkeys from their mother one hour a day, which, as you can imagine, was a stressful experience for the monkeys. The researchers therefore expected this would lead to emotional imbalance, but quite surprisingly the opposite was the case: the monkeys separated from their mother at a young age developed more resilience than monkeys that were allowed to hang with mum all day. The monkeys from the first group showed greater resilience and curiosity even as adults. The researchers also looked at the changes in the brain. And what did they find? The monkeys who had been separated from their mothers early on developed a larger prefrontal cortex. In particular, the areas that temper fear responses, improve impulse control and increase positive motivation were better developed than those who had not been separated.

Although research on this so-called neuroplasticity has many mysteries yet to solve, we already know a lot about it as well. Here is a summary of the main findings.

Your brain has the capacity to re-activate pathways that have been inactive for a long period of time

You never unlearn a skill once acquired, although it may need some practice to get those neurons back to cruising speed. Unfortunately this also applies to skills we'd be better off without, such as having panic attacks driving down the motorway. This is also something I notice in some people's stories: they are aware of all sorts of symptoms and phenomena even long after their burn-out and sometimes it takes years before they suddenly realise: "Wait a minute, I've been driving around without being worried about having a panic attack!"

Your brain is able to make new pathways

Your neurons are renewed every few weeks. When you learn something new, your brain is able to strengthen existing nerve connections or make new ones. Two substances are crucial here: serotonin and dopamine. They boost your motivation and increase your sense of self-confidence and power. You can stimulate the production and flow of these two neurotransmitters by getting enough sleep and doing activities that relax you and make you feel good about yourself. Another way to facilitate this is to build up a mental reserve (see exercise 24).

Your brain can rebuild pathways

Part of your brain that was used in the past for a certain task can later be used for something else, for example, after a stroke. After a part of the brain is damaged, a different part of your brain might be able to assume responsibility for that activity. The younger the person suffering from a brain injury, the better the chances for recovery, however, even as we age, our brains remain surprisingly flexible.

Your brain can shut down deviating circuits and connections

Some parts of your brain can control other parts that are causing you to change your mood, decisions, or thoughts. This means you can influence your stress patterns with your own actions. You can help your brain set off fewer alarm signals, thus decreasing your symptoms and allowing yourself once again to get a handle on what is happening. No matter how you ask your brain something (consciously, focused, with exercise and confirmation), it will try to execute it. And the more you ask your brain to think of something pleasant, the more your brain will react to it.

EXERCISE
Increase
your mental
reserve

Make a list of the things you would still like to do. You could split up the list into two columns, one headed 'work' and one headed 'private'. Under 'work', you could then further differentiate between what you still would like to try with your current job/employer and what you would like to do later in your professional life.

When your list is finished, see which items could be done right away and which ones might require more time. Then choose those activities you are excited about and will challenge you intellectually, but which are also achievable in less than day or no more than three separate hours in a week. Schedule the time to work on it and persevere!

Our stress response:
ON/OFF and the need for recovery time

What happens in our brain and the rest of our body when we experience stress? Simply put, our stress response lets us handle more than we thought possible. We rise to the challenge! Figure 1 shows how our stress response can increase our capacity to achieve.

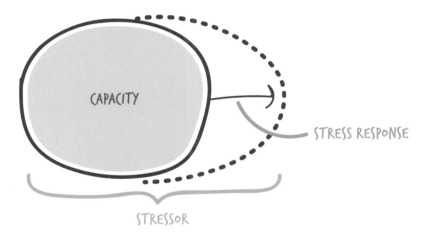

FIGURE 1 / Stress response ensures that we can do more than we thought.

A healthy stress response is short and powerful. Anatomically speaking, your stress system runs from your brain to your adrenal glands (near the small of your back). The adrenal glands release adrenaline and cortisol, two hormones that keep you ready for action. This is also called the fight-flight-freeze response with your body in a heightened state of preparedness. The so-called sympathetic nervous system is activated and ensures your body mobilizes energy. Your heart rate increases to get more oxygen and energy to your muscles and brain.

Adrenaline also sharpens your senses. Your pupils dilate to let more light in and your hearing becomes more acute. Your brain will also process observations more quickly. Activities that are less important at that moment will be postponed, such as digesting food or daydreaming. The chemical cocktail of endorphins, adrenaline, testosterone and dopamine also gives your motivation a boost. It gives you a light rush and increases your sense of self-confidence and strength. (This is one aspect of stress that some people enjoy and even become addicted to.) To sum it up, the stress response prepares your body and your mind to take on the challenge and to stretch your physical and mental boundaries.

EXERCISE
Reflection
after a stress
peak

After a stress peak you should give your brain some recovery time to rewire. If you don't, you run the risk of another breakdown happening soon.

This exercise may help:

▼ Reflect on what happened once the stress peak has passed.

▼ Assess the severity of the peak on a scale from 1 to 10 (1 being no stress whatsoever, 10 being the worst stress imaginable).

▼ How did you deal with this situation? What did you do to overcome the stress?

▼ What can you learn from this to apply to future stress peaks?

After a stress peak, the stress response subsides. This is also part of the recovery process. Your body has hormones stored up to help you through this. However, this requires time to recover from the stress peak. A few hours after experiencing a strong stress response, your brain will still be trying to rewire itself in order to remember the experience and learn from it. During this time, stress hormones increase the activity in those areas of the brain that support learning and memory. The high emotions that can be experienced at this time are all a part of the process the brain uses to try and figure out the experience. Do you remember your last stress peak? You may have felt weak in the knees right after, you might have needed to cry, or felt a powerful sense of excitement. These are all signs that the stress system wants to activate all those areas needed to comprehend what just happened.

TEST / HOW BIG IS YOUR NEED FOR RECOVERY?[1]

Answer the following questions by indicating how you feel, on average, after a day at work.

1 *At the end of the workday I find it difficult to relax.*
   1 ○ yes 0 ○ no

2 *At the end of a workday I'm really done.*
   1 ○ yes 0 ○ no

3 *My work causes me to feel rather exhausted at the end of a work day.*
   1 ○ yes 0 ○ no

4 *After dinner, I usually still feel quite energetic.*
   0 ○ yes 1 ○ no

5 *I usually only start unwinding on the second day off.*
   1 ○ yes 0 ○ no

6 *I find it hard to concentrate during my free time after work.*
   1 ○ yes 0 ○ no

7 *I have little interest in others after arriving home from work.*
   1 ○ yes 0 ○ no

8 *In general it takes me more than one hour to completely recover after work.*
   1 ○ yes 0 ○ no

1 These questions are part of the *Vragenlijst Beleving en Beoordeling van de Arbeid* (Questionnaire on the Perception and Assessment of Work), developed in the Netherlands by the Stichting Kwaliteitsbevordering Bedrijfsgezondheidszorg (SKB, Organisation for the Promotion of Quality in Occupational Health).

9 *When I come home from work, I want everyone to leave me alone for just a little bit.*

      1 ○ yes 0 ○ no

10 *It often happens that I'm so tired when I come home that I can't do anything else after work.*

      1 ○ yes 0 ○ no

11 *It often happens that I am so tired the last few hours of my workday that I can't do my work.*

      1 ○ yes 0 ○ no

Scoring your need for recovery

More than 5 (out of 11)

You have an increased need for recovery. This means that, if the current situation in your private life or work environment persists, you will have an increased risk of developing problems with your mental health. We advise you to contact your HR department, your GP, the company doctor, or the mental health consultant at work.

5 or less

You do not have an increased need for recovery which means you do not currently have an increased risk of developing mental health issues.

Contrary to what most people think, your body can react to stress in many different ways. The psychological and social consequences may also differ from person to person. However, broadly speaking, we can distinguish three types of stress responses, each of which handles stress in a different way.

The fight-flight-freeze response
If your life is at stake (or seems to be, for it makes no difference to your brain), the fight-flight-freeze response will be triggered. It provides energy and allows for extraordinary physical performance.

> **TIP /** STOMPING YOUR FEET
>
> Do you feel completely overwrought? Can't get rid of that feeling? Go for a walk. Go outside and stomp your feet really hard. Your hormones are demanding a physical response, so give them one.

The challenge response
When a stressor is less threatening, the brain and body will go into a challenge response. Just like the fight-flight-freeze response, the challenge response gives you energy and helps you to perform under pressure. However, there are a few big differences: you will feel more focused than afraid, for example. A challenge response will increase self-confidence, encourage action, and help you to learn from experience. This challenge response is associated with the concept of being 'in flow'. This does not mean being physiologically calm, but you are instead experiencing a challenge response, which boosts your self-confidence and increases your concentration. The Framingham Heart Study, one of the longest-running health studies in the world, has shown that people with a challenge response maintained greater brain capacity as they aged. The fastest way to shift to this response from a classic fight-flight-freeze response is to be curious. Once you are curious, you will no longer be able respond with fear.

Make a list of your personal triggers. When have you reached your limit? How do you know you've reached your limit? Be honest with yourself and thoroughly observe how you respond to things. Distinguish between the signals of your body and when your colleagues cause you stress. Take a time-out when the alarm signals appear.

The nurture-and-befriend response

Your stress response not only gives you energy. In many circumstances, stress also encourages you to connect with others. This response is mainly driven by oxytocin, also called the hugging hormone. Oxytocin increases your empathy and intuition, but also suppresses your fears. This hormone reduces the fear response in your brain and thus suppresses the instinct to freeze or flee. In short, it makes you more receptive to others. This is all due to the nurture-and-befriend response, which of course plays a very important role in forming relationships both at home and at work. It increases your courage, prompts caring, and strengthens social relationships.

TIP / SAY "HELLO!"

Say something sincerely nice to a colleague, friend, or even a casual passer-by. Don't know what to say? Keep a book with interesting facts to fall back on during a conversation. For instance, I remind myself to ask how a colleague's child is doing after an illness. Or maybe surprise someone with a nice gift.

Like a headless chicken

So if stress is a natural, normal and healthy warning signal, why do so many people suffer from stress-related symptoms? Why is stress causing so many people to literally become ill?

To use stress to your advantage, you should first become aware of when and why you get stressed. And you should know your limits. That's usually the rub. We can handle stress in short peaks. If our brakes work well in such cases, our system will relax again after a stressor. However, sometimes there is such a rapid succession of efforts that we are unable to erase all the traces of stress. The result: stress accumulates and we begin to say we suffer from chronic stress. It's like your accelerator has gotten stuck or your brakes are failing and you are no longer producing recovery hormones and your batteries are slowly but surely depleting.

The Apgar score is a number from 1 to 10 used in neonatology to assess the health of new-born babies. Apgar stands for appearance, pulse, grimace (reflex irritability), activity and respiration. In other words: does the baby have a healthy colour, is the heartbeat and muscle tension OK, does the baby react to stimuli, and does the baby breathe well?
To find out if you are dealing with toxic stress you can use an alternate Apgar test. Use the following questionnaire to keep your finger on the pulse. When more than two of the following five domains **suddenly** *change, it's time to take action.*

○ *Appearance: is there a sudden change in your look, weight, sleeping pattern, (medical) substance use...?*

○ *Performance: do you feel you are suddenly under-performing or over-performing?*

○ *Growth tension: are you able and willing to take on new information?*

○ *Affect control: are you able to control your emotions and frustrations?*

○ *Relationships: is there a sudden noticeable change in social interaction?*

Please note that this test has no diagnostic value whatsoever. It is merely a tool to help recognize the proverbial straw that will break the camel's back in a timely manner.

Physical effort puts more pressure on the accelerator, while relaxation and breathing exercises push down the brake. Every time you take a deep breath, the accelerator is activated. The adrenaline released by this accelerates your heartbeat. Exhaling activates the brake: your heartbeat slows down. While breathing we are therefore continuously speeding up and slowing down. That is why so many disciplines pay so much attention to breathing, for example yoga or Pilates.

EXERCISE
4-7-8
breathing
technique

Every time you take a deep breath, you press down on your body's accelerator, releasing adrenaline that accelerates your heartbeat. Exhaling activates the brake and your heartbeat slows down. While breathing, you are therefore continuously speeding up and slowing down. It is no coincidence that yoga and Pilates, for example, pay a lot of attention to breathing techniques.

To deliberately slow down, you could try the 4-7-8 breathing technique:
▼ Inhale to a count of 4.
▼ Hold your breath for a count of 7.
▼ Exhale to a count of 8.

You could also alternate with the 4-7-8-STOP breathing technique. This is where you wait right after exhaling and before you inhale again to a count of 4.

Do the 4-7-8 breathing technique a maximum of five times in a row.

Afterwards you will often hear people say in amazement: "I had no idea!" Why is this the case? We are just like that frog sitting in a pan of water slowly brought to a boil. It will stay there until it is completely cooked. If you are headed for burnout, basically the same thing will happen: as your stress slowly builds up without being released, you won't notice when it's ready to boil over.

It's therefore good to pay attention to the signals your family, friends, or colleagues send. They are often the first ones to notice you are not doing well. Too many of us ignore these warnings, however. One of the problems is that when you are no longer able to gauge your stress level, you will no longer want to or even be able to listen.

TIP / SCHEDULE DOWNTIME

If you want to produce more recovery hormones, schedule regular downtime. Just do nothing, do something completely different, or just daydream. For example think of a pleasant situation that occurred not so long ago, dream of all the things you still want to do in your life, or daydream about a place where you can fully relax and enjoy the moment for a while. Set aside some time for this during your workday or even have your phone send you an automated reminder.

All sorts of things are happening in your brain that make it really difficult to properly assess your stress. The culprit is your prefrontal cortex, located behind your forehead. The prefrontal cortex can be described as the cockpit of your brain, the place where all (or at least a lot) of information is gathered, so that you can plan, put things in perspective, understand nuance, make decisions, regulate emotions... If the prefrontal cortex no longer functions properly, all sorts of problems will arise. People who are under toxic stress start behaving differently. They become more impulsive, ask or even cry for help and support, experience less freedom and more pain. These are all signals telling your body that your current situation is slowly becoming untenable.

TIP / TAMING YOUR 'HEADLESS CHICKEN'

A simple tip to take control of your 'headless chicken' is ice. Hold a cold pack (one of those blue bags you put in the freezer) in your hands until you have become calm again. This will give your stress system a chance to recover. (If you are curious about the science behind this tip, Google 'the ice man'.) At the same time, be aware that you don't need to panic, but that it's just your 'headless chicken' playing tricks on you. Don't worry if at first you don't succeed. Just try and try again. Practice makes perfect.

Normally there is an excellent connection between our prefrontal cortex and our stress brain. (This stress brain is not a purely anatomical part of our brain, but a combination of our reptilian brain and the limbic system which is responsible for emotions.) Except when things are about to get out of hand, then your stress brain takes over. The result: you are at the mercy of the emotional part of your brain and you're running around like a head-less chicken. This can be accompanied by physical symptoms such as hyperventilation, muscle pain, shaking, confusion, or shaky legs.

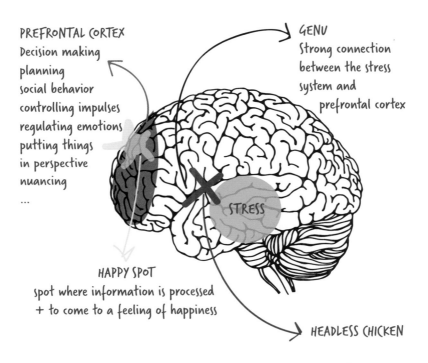

PREFRONTAL CORTEX
Decision making
planning
social behavior
controlling impulses
regulating emotions
putting things
in perspective
nuancing
...

GENU
Strong connection
between the stress
system and
prefrontal cortex

STRESS

HAPPY SPOT
spot where information is processed
+ to come to a feeling of happiness

HEADLESS CHICKEN

FIGURE 2 / When our prefrontal cortex and our stress system are no longer aligned, we start behaving like a headless chicken.

Especially the role of the **genu** is interesting here. It is presumed that positive emotions (for example comfort) can reduce pain and stress via this area by producing recovery hormones. Negative emotions (such as fear) through the genu area however increase pain and stress. In addition, research has also shown that our brain turns off part of our memory when danger looms, in particular that part of the hippocampus involved with new facts and knowledge. In other words, in case of imminent danger we no longer focus on the here and now. For example, every time I see a black Labrador, I am inevitably reminded of the black Labrador that bit me when I was ten years old. This reflex offers protection: it makes me jump back, making sure I am

37

safe. But in other, completely safe situations this reflex no longer has a function and it only causes problems.

TIP / MAKE THE WORLD LESS THREATENING

Keeping the knowledge of the different stress responses in mind, the following tips can help make the world around you less threatening.

- ○ Meet a friend and tell him/her about your experiences and invite him/her to help you.
- ○ If you see a colleague in distress, take action and help out. This could mean actively helping, but also by just talking to this person or by surprising this person with a small gift.
- ○ Immediately discuss injustices, otherwise it could put your group feeling at risk.
  - ▼ Think about what you feel is unfair.
  - ▼ Ask yourself why this is so important to you.
  - ▼ Check how you will see that it is going well (that the unfairness is no longer present).
  - ▼ What is your role in this?
  - ▼ Express clear expectations.
- ○ Think about how your stress can help your team. What lessons can your colleagues learn from your stressful experience?

Resilience means, as we will see in the next chapter, the ability to reduce the duration and impact of the negative emotion. When the prefrontal cortex takes the time to process a negative emotion with the help of the genu area, the activity in our fear centre will decrease. The processing time may be a measure for the resilience and psychological well-being. If our brain does not receive that time, fewer and fewer recovery hormones are released, which again affects stress and pain.

Other researchers showed that even after the toxicity of stress disappeared, both the genu area and our fear centre remain more sensitive to negative emotions. You will respond with the same intensity to increasingly smaller stimuli. Your entire system becomes hypersensitive and the least amount of headwind will blow you down.

That is why it is so important to work on your resilience on a regular basis. It is not enough to do the exercises in this book faithfully for a few months and when your symptoms have disappeared to pick up where you left off. Your brain requires regular maintenance. So try to give these exercises a permanent place in your life.

EXERCISE
Create a weekly overview

Create an overview of your week. What is the best time of the day to spend ten minutes on building your resilience? Lock in this time. Consider this time as a non-negotiable rule! When do you have an extra 15 minutes of time during the week to evaluate the progress you are making? Write down these times in your planner and make this time non-negotiable as well.

It is also interesting that the genu is very sensitive to rewards. Focusing on the desired positive result keeps this area active. If you don't like the situation you are currently in, then what is it that you want? The better you can describe this, the better the genu will work to your advantage. You can find out more about this in chapter 4.

A good way to expand the power of your prefrontal cortex is to put together a 'Wow, I'm great!' folder, making an external back-up of your happy feelings, as it were. How? Find all positive feedback, nice gifts, thank you cards, reference letters, compliments and so on and keep them in one folder. Highlight the positive messages so they stand out. Of course, this can be done digitally as well. Save all emails with compliments in a 'wow' folder, or take a picture with your smart phone and save it in your 'feeling good' folder. Use these folders when you don't feel as great about yourself, when you need a pick-me-up or when you can't find a solution to a specific challenge. Don't let your folder collect dust. Instead, take a look at it at least once a week.

And there is good news too: by keeping the bar low, you can turn this over-sensitivity around. This also explains why having structure in your daily life is so important to climb out of the valley of stress. This is how you make sure that the genu slowly learns how to take control of its function again. On the other hand, when we subconsciously (continue to) set the bar too high, i.e. want more than we can handle, the disruption will only become bigger and our over-sensitivity will increase.

EXERCISE
The 'stress champ' of the week

Schedule a round of 'stress champ' every week. During this activity, each person should tell his or her worst experience with stress in the past week. Vote together to decide who is the stress champ of the week. Regardless of whether the stress champ was able to eliminate the negative stress, everyone discusses how best to deal with the stress experience, both as a team and as an individual. This way your team can tap into new resources before stress takes place.
Conclude the session as follows: the stress champ faces the wall. The other team members say as many positive things about him/her as possible. Of course, you can also do this exercise at home with your family members or even in a group session during therapy.

If you dig a pit...

When the stress brain takes over our brain, a lot happens with our thoughts. The pilot in the cockpit (your prefrontal cortex) can no longer keep control over the stress brain due to faulty wiring connecting to the stress brain. It's just like a stuck flap on an aeroplane. Now that the pilot is no longer able to fly, our auto-pilot takes over. Before we know it, we fall into the many traps of our own making. Living on auto-pilot:

- causes us not to be aware of our stress level;
- causes us not to be able to use our stress to our advantage;
- has us seeing things that aren't there, focusing on what we don't have and on what is going wrong;
- creates an ideal breeding ground for the negative effects of stress.

When our prefrontal cortex and our stress brain no longer cooperate, we also tend to register emotions as physical complaints. Simply put, instead of experiencing and seeing our emotions as a signal that something is off, we experience intestinal problems, we have migraines, or heart palpitations.

From a young age, we taught ourselves techniques to deal with stress. As we grow older, we continue to hold on to these patterns, even if they are anything but efficient. If, as a child, you found comfort in candy, as an adult you may reach for an extra slice of pizza or an extra glass of wine. Even the sensitivities from your childhood will re-emerge during moments of peak stress. If, as a child, you had the feeling that whatever you did was never good enough, then there is a good chance that you will experience that same feeling as an adult when under pressure. That's why we often feel angry, sad or anxious when we are under extreme stress. These emotions will, in turn, taint the way we look at the world, and will put us in a vicious circle. Because when these pitfalls are (overly) active, they will start to steer the way we look at the world. In other words, we look for proof for our thoughts and get stuck in self-fulfilling prophecies.

To summarise, too much stress will:

- cause an increasingly stronger activation of the stress system;
- make you lose the link between your stress system and your prefrontal cortex ('headless chicken');
- make your pitfalls more prominent;
- make you less flexible in your way of thinking: your point of view is the truth!

EXERCISE
Listening to each other

will get more confidence in your ability to deal with the challenges of life. You are creating a strong network of social support. Controllable problems are resolved instead of letting them get out of hand. Uncontrollable situations become chances to grow. You don't need to do this by yourself. Shall we take a look at what is going on here?

Help your colleague/partner/friend/family member by taking away the threatening element of stress. Listen to their story. Normalise. The following text can help you with this. *Everyone has their own opinion about stress. Each time you experience stress, your preconceived notions about it will come to mind. These notions can either help you or not. When you face the difficulties instead of ignoring or denying them, you will build resources to deal with stressful situations. You*

Listen. Suggest to the other person to see when he/she experienced something similar in the past. How did he/she handle that situation?
This solution, can it be applied to this case as well? How? What do you need in order to do so? How can I help you? How will we see that we are on the right track?

After this conversation, schedule a time to come together and check if things are better.

It's not surprising that when we experience stress it is even harder to listen to the signals of our body. The more stress we experience, the more rigid our thoughts. We are no longer able to investigate other perspectives or points of view. However this is important if we are going to break the negative spiral. This also explains why people with a lot of stress have a hard time trying to get out of the slump they are in. It has nothing to do with their willpower or perseverance; instead, it has to do with their lack of flexibility in the way they think.

If you are completely stuck in a rut, you will only function through instinctive thinking patterns and reflexes. You will not be able to make any conscious decisions. Having this pointed out to us won't do any good, since our brain areas are no longer in tune. This can cause us to be gripped by fear, ignorance and insecurity. We become dependent or passive towards our environment. Instead of finding a fitting solution for each situation, we continue to use the same actions, even if they have previously proved to be unsuccessful. Toxic stress causes the mental flexibility so vital to our sense of imagination to disappear. Instead, you keep playing the same film, over and over, and you can't find any (new) solutions.

And it goes on. Under the influence of toxic stress, most people will start to re-enact or churn through the situation, desperately trying to find a solution. This re-enactment, however, can't work because these are rigid scenarios that can barely change, if at all. This is in contrast to our normal memories, which are adaptive. Our stories are flexible and can be adjusted to the circumstances. This is not the case when 'milling': it's always the same story. The first step then is to stabilize your stress system. It is my experience that once the symptoms are stabilised, these re-enactments spontaneously disappear and the new-found imagination and creativity lead to new insights and progress.

The stress continuum: the highway to hell

Although stress symptoms (and ultimately burn-out) seem to creep up on you without noticing, there are alarm signals that will give you a wake-up call. The many stories from people with stress-related problems show that you don't become burnt-out overnight. That's why we talk about a stress continuum, running from 'regular' stress (which each of us experiences) to total burn-out (at the extreme right of the spectrum).

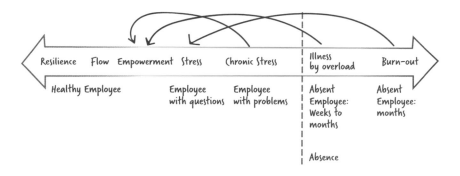

FIGURE 3 / The stress continuum: from 'regular' stress to total burn-out. Each phase has alarm signals, but many people manage to ignore them.

Everyone experiences stress, even the most resilient people. As we have already seen, this is good and even necessary; stress is a healthy warning signal. However, if you are not well aware of it or if stress builds up, you will slowly slide to the right on the stress continuum.

TIP / START YOUR WORKDAY DIFFERENTLY

Start your day with one hour of work without opening your email, one hour in which your colleagues or customers cannot disturb you. This will let you finish an important assignment and start your day with a successful experience.

At first you are a bit **tense**. Your fuse is getting shorter and you become increasingly thin-skinned. You mostly see problems. You lack time, you aren't sleeping as well, and you feel more anxious than usual. Maybe you are also suffering from headaches, muscle tension, or neck pain.

If the situation persists, you will have **chronic stress**. The first physical symptoms appear and will start to hinder you. This is often the phase where people start taking medication to take care of the symptoms. Maybe you have already paid a visit to your GP for 'separate' symptoms: not sleeping well, stomach and intestinal issues, infections, being tired and lethargic, not being able to relax while on holidays... You become increasingly irritated, you have already told off your colleagues or friends and maybe you are experiencing panic attacks. The people in your environment start to notice that something has changed and will spontaneously start to encourage you or spontaneously help you with one thing or another. Your colleagues or people in your immediate surrounding begin saying something to you about your changed behaviour.

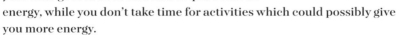

You slowly come to the point where all the alarm signals should start going off. By now, the symptoms are definitely serious, but you can still make it out of the slump on your own. The changes continue as you move in the wrong direction on the stress continuum and you become **exhausted**. Your exhaustion now causes you to also start adjusting your social life. You put your hobbies on the back burner in order to continue to function at work. All your time goes to activities that require a lot of energy, while you don't take time for activities which could possibly give you more energy.

Chronic stress slowly evolves into utter exhaustion and depression. You become cynical. "What does it matter? Nothing will change anyway!" Or you start acting like Ambrose, from the Spike and Suzy comics: you become angry before the problems appear. Your anger no longer correlates to the facts. Your emotions start taking over. Please note: depression is not the same as burn-out. Depression is a mood disturbance, burn-out is an energy disturbance. Simply put, a person with depression does not see 'the use', but is still physically going, while someone with burn-out has the opposite: he or she wants to, but can't go on physically because they are completely exhausted.

Slowly, but surely your brain is getting fried. It no longer functions like it should. Everything requires lots of effort and time. Your results are not what you were used to. You drag yourself from one thing to the next. Exhaustion and emotional emptiness plus cynicism plus decreased personal competence are key symptoms of burn-out. The other areas of your life might still going well. This may mean you are experiencing **burn-out in one role**. For example, you may no longer be functioning at work, but you keep strong in your family. An important symptom here is confusion. Because of the difficulty concentrating, it is hard to follow conversations. It skips from one subject to another and is easily distracted. This is not a personality trait, but a temporary phenomenon.

It's a small step from burn-out in one role to a **complete burn-out** where all the lights go out. At that point, nothing else works. You no longer see any perspective or possibilities and your screen goes blank.

1 *How often does it happen that you are no longer able to perform your job properly due to things out of your control (e.g. imposed time pressure, frequent unexpected extra assignments, useless tasks, private circumstances)?*

4 ○ very often/constantly
3 ○ often
2 ○ occasionally
1 ○ rarely
0 ○ never/hardly ever

2 *During the past four weeks, how often did you feel worn out?*

4 ○ very often/constantly
3 ○ a big portion of the time
2 ○ a portion of the time
1 ○ a small portion of the time
0 ○ not at all

3 *During the past four weeks, how often did you feel emotionally exhausted?*

4 ○ very often/constantly
3 ○ a big portion of the time
2 ○ a portion of the time
1 ○ a small portion of the time
0 ○ not at all

4 *During the past four weeks, how often did you feel physically exhausted?*

4 ○ very often/constantly
3 ○ a big portion of the time
2 ○ a portion of the time
1 ○ a small portion of the time
0 ○ not at all

5 *During the past four weeks, how often did you feel tired?*

4 ○ very often/constantly
3 ○ a big portion of the time
2 ○ a portion of the time
1 ○ a small portion of the time
0 ○ not at all

6 *During the past four weeks, how often was it harder than usual for you to concentrate?*

4 ○ very often/constantly
3 ○ often
2 ○ occasionally
1 ○ rarely
0 ○ never/hardly ever

7 *During the past four weeks, how often was it harder than usual to think clearly?*

4 ○ very often/constantly
3 ○ often
2 ○ occasionally
1 ○ rarely
0 ○ never/hardly ever

8 *During the past for weeks, how often was it harder than usual to make a decision?*

4 ○ very often/constantly
3 ○ often
2 ○ occasionally
1 ○ rarely
0 ○ never/hardly ever

9 During the past for weeks, how often was it harder than usual to remember something?

4 ○ very often/constantly
3 ○ often
2 ○ occasionally
1 ○ rarely
0 ○ never/hardly ever

10 During the past four weeks at work, how often did you become irritated faster than usual?

4 ○ very often/constantly
3 ○ often
2 ○ regularly
1 ○ occasionally
0 ○ never/hardly ever

11 During the past four weeks at work, how often did you become emotional faster than usual?

4 ○ very often/constantly
3 ○ often
2 ○ regularly
1 ○ occasionally
0 ○ never/hardly ever

12 During the past four weeks, how often did you have sleeping problems (lying awake for a long period of time and/or waking up much too early)?

4 ○ very often/constantly
3 ○ often
2 ○ regularly
1 ○ occasionally
0 ○ never/hardly ever

13 *During the past four weeks, how often did you doubt whether you are able to do your job?*

4 ○ very often/constantly
3 ○ often
2 ○ regularly
1 ○ occasionally
0 ○ never/hardly ever

14 *During the past four weeks, how often did you doubt whether your job is useful?*

4 ○ very often/constantly
3 ○ often
2 ○ regularly
1 ○ occasionally
0 ○ never/hardly ever

GLOBAL BURN-OUT SCORE

19 or less (out of 56)

There are currently no indications you have an increased risk for developing burn-out.

20 to 26

Your answers indicate that if the current situation persists you could end up in a situation with an increased risk for developing burn-out. We advise you to contact your GP, the company doctor, or a mental health professional.

27 or more

Your answers indicate that currently there is an increased risk for developing burn-out. We advise you to contact your GP, the company doctor, or a mental health professional.

Summary

○ Stress is a signal that indicates the need for change.
○ If you practice handling stress at a time you are not yet experiencing its negative effects of stress, you will be able to make better use of stress to your advantage.
○ Stress contributes to a vibrant brain.
○ Being aware of your stress level is already a good buffer for the negative effects of stress.

What will you remember from this chapter?

_____

_____

_____

_____

_____

New insights:

_____

_____

_____

_____

_____

How will you set out to do this?

_____

_____

_____

_____

_____

2/ Focus on resilience and growth

As soon as stress enters the toxic phase, you try to avoid pain as much as possible. As a result you become overheated in situations which previously you were able to handle relatively well. This in turn leads to avoidance (*fear of failure*) and excessive or compulsive control of the environment (maladaptive perfectionism). When our stress system and our cockpit are in tune, we can speak of **resilience**. But in order to expand this resilience your focus should be on **growth** as much as possible. This means you should focus on how to move forward, instead of wondering what all went wrong in the past.

Maybe this focus on growth seems a bit dreamy. Keep in mind however, that growth is not about an alternative type of idealism, but is a necessity, pure and simple, both in our personal and social lives. Growth enables us to better cope with the fast moving changes in our society and with increasing demands for productivity. Growth is therefore a necessary tool to function well in our current society.

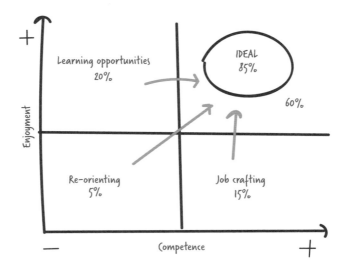

EXERCISE

The ideal quadrant

Take a look at your assignments. What do you enjoy doing? What assignments do you enjoy? Which areas do you feel competent in? Put these two parameters in a diagram with four quadrants. Ideally, 85 percent of your work time should be spent on things from the ideal quadrant: tasks you enjoy doing and which you are competent at. Of course, no job is just fun-fun-fun, nevertheless you should be able to ask yourself what you can do to move it to the ideal quadrant.

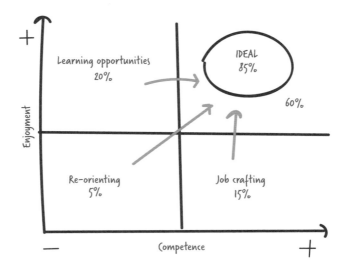

All your tasks and responsibilities can be placed in these quadrants. Next, examine how the tasks from the three other quadrants can be adapted to move towards the ideal quadrant. Tasks you enjoy doing, but for which you do not feel competent yet can be honed through learning opportunities. Tasks you feel competent in, but which you do not particularly like, could still move towards the ideal quadrant by looking at them from a different angle or by organising them differently. That is called *job crafting*: literally altering your job in the direction of the ideal. The only quadrant that should be or become as empty as possible is the bottom left quadrant: the tasks you do not enjoy doing and in which you feel incompetent.

Discover your own compass

In the past ten years we have received some clear insight from the angle of positive psychology on why it is so important to experience success in different areas of life. Research is focusing more and more on the question of what the mechanisms and processes of optimal functioning are, instead of just focusing on the mechanisms of dysfunction. One of the pioneers in this study is Ed Diener, also known as Dr. Happiness. His research does not focus on what all can go wrong, rather he wants to know which aspects of our life make us happy and successful and allow us to flourish. The underlying idea (and this is confirmed in many studies) is that happiness and success influence each other in both directions. Success makes people happier, but conversely, being happy also makes for more success. It isn't necessarily objectively measurable success: it's not the number of degrees hanging on your wall or the amount of money in your bank account that count, but rather how you assess your success yourself.

TIP / PREPARING FOR A PERFORMANCE REVIEW

A performance review at work can bring about a lot of stress. However, it shouldn't be that way. On the contrary, it should be the ideal opportunity to align the employer's expectations with yours more clearly. Moreover, if you prepare for the review, there's no reason to enter it with your knees shaking. The following questions can help.

○ Find out what your most important successes have been.
○ What are your personal qualities, your strengths?
○ In what other way can you also use these strengths?
○ What else would you like to do in your job?
The exercise 'Positive time travel', later in this chapter, can help to prepare for a performance review as well.

The World Health Organization defines mental health in a positive way as 'a subjective state of well-being in which the individual realizes his or her own full potential in his or her life and in his or her community'. From the work of leading psychologists focusing on human growth and development, Carol Ryff found a number of criteria that are essential to realising your own potential. Each is in its own way important for a happy and resilient life: purpose in life, personal growth, autonomy, controlling your environment, self-acceptance, and positive relationships.

Based on these elements we can conclude that self-acceptance and intimacy in social relationships are two important conditions for freely choosing a path in life which contributes to personal growth and development. In other words, it is the basis for achieving your full potential.

Purpose in life
This domain includes the following aspects:
○ I find a certain meaning in my life that gives me satisfaction.
○ I reach most of my goals.
○ I am on track to realising my dreams.

Personal growth
This domain includes the following aspects:
○ Learning new things is important to me.
○ I learned something new yesterday.
○ I learn something new every day.

Autonomy

This domain includes the following aspects:

- ○ I can plan my tasks mostly by myself.
- ○ I am allowed to make decisions and do not need to ask my partner/boss for permission for everything.
- ○ I do not need pressure from others to motivate myself (intrinsic motivation).

Controlling your environment

This domain includes the following aspects:

- ○ I often utilise my skills in my daily life.
- ○ I believe I'm good at most things.
- ○ I expect more good things than bad ones on my path.

Self-acceptance

This domain includes the following aspects:

- ○ I am usually positive.
- ○ I am satisfied with my life.
- ○ I am optimistic about my future.

Positive relationships

This domain includes the following aspects:

- ○ There are people I can count on for help.
- ○ I feel I am a part of my community.
- ○ There are people who appreciate me for who I am.

EXERCISE
Make your own spider diagram

Take a moment to reflect on these domains. How successful have you been in realising these domains? Assign a value to each domain on a scale from 0 (= not going well at all) to 10 (= I feel great in this area).

How successful do you feel in knowing the purpose of your life?

0   1   2   3   4   5   6   7   8   9   10

How successful do you feel in personal growth?

0   1   2   3   4   5   6   7   8   9   10

How successful do you feel at being autonomous?

0   1   2   3   4   5   6   7   8   9   10

How successful do you feel in controlling your environment?

0   1   2   3   4   5   6   7   8   9   10

How successful do you feel at accepting yourself?

0   1   2   3   4   5   6   7   8   9   10

How successful do you feel at nurturing positive relationships?

0   1   2   3   4   5   6   7   8   9   10

You have now assigned a personal score to each of these pillars. Summarise them in the spider diagram below. You will see at a glance where you stand and which domains still need some work.

EXERCISE
Where are you
now and where
do you want
to be?

Where are you now and where do you want to be on a scale from 1 (= very dissatisfied) to 10 (= completely satisfied)? Why do you give yourself that score? What would you need in order to go up a point? Do this exercise for each domain as necessary.

Increase your resilience

As mentioned earlier, stress prepares our body for change. But quite often we don't want change! By nature, we are creatures of habit geared to security and stability. In order to survive, our distant ancestors had to stay close to their cave. If they ventured into unknown territory, the risk of danger increased, which could jeopardise the survival of the entire family.

TIP / Look for fixed rituals

Make sure there is a set structure that always returns. Rituals create peace and predictability and calm our stress system. Especially if you have young children, routine and structure are very important. Especially during the morning and evening rush, as a parent do yourself a favour and let your children know in advance what is expected of them. But even if you don't have children, you can benefit from some regularity in life. This shouldn't be boring at all, as long as you don't live a strictly regimented life.

Of course, sometimes things don't go the way they're supposed to, but don't worry: there's always tomorrow. Sometimes what seems impossible is merely difficult. And then it's just a matter of persevering.

Is it starting to get harder when you attempt to keep stress under control and expand your resilience? Are you having doubts, insecurities, or even negative emotions? Such reactions are not uncommon. It is your brain trying to tell you that it is not indifferent to these changes. The brain is involved and you should use this involvement to your advantage. By always having a clear view of what you are doing, why you are taking these steps, and where they are leading (as defined in your action plan), you will be able to gradually suppress these negative emotions. Resilient people:

- usually have stable relationship;
- are working on developing themselves;
- have goals to aspire to in both their private and professional lives;
- score higher in the area of psychological well-being.

TIPS / HOW TO STIMULATE POSITIVE EMOTIONS

- **Use your strengths.** Map out your talents and qualities, with or without questionnaires. Think about how you can increase the use of these talents in your daily life.
- Every day, reflect on **three positive events** that happened to you that day and write them down. Read this the next day before getting up. Try to recall these events.
- **Express your gratitude.** Think of someone you should thank, someone you have not yet properly thanked in one way or another. Write a letter to that person.
- React at least once a day in an **enthusiastic and active** way to a positive message from someone. For example, thank them for a compliment or reply with a nice message.

○ **Enjoy!** Your assignment is deceptively simple: try to enjoy an activity that you would normally perform in a hurry. Afterwards, describe what was different and how you felt about it.

Working on your psychological well-being is more than just eliminating all sorts of symptoms and disorders https://www.lannoo.be/nl/eerste-hulp-bij-nieuwe-gezinnen. It also involves optimal functioning. In other words, you don't just want to go from -3 to 0, you also want to achieve level +3.

In that respect, it is interesting to delve a bit deeper into the work of Barbara Fredrickson. Her **broaden-and-build theory** laid the foundation for many interventions which we now apply in practice. According to this theory, positive emotions lead to optimal functioning: they broaden the scope of attention, cognition and action. In addition, positive emotions also build sustainable resources, not only physical and cognitive but also social. People who experience positive emotions think differently than people who experience neutral or negative emotions:

○ They are more open to information and can also process this information better.
○ They are less self-centred and experience a greater connectedness to others.
○ It is easier for them to interact socially and they are more helpful.
○ They have a healthier lifestyle, reducing the risk of diseases.

It is therefore important to stimulate positive emotions, since that's where it all starts.

EXERCISE
Positive Time Travel

Describe your ten most beautiful memories, your ten biggest successes and the ten most beautiful moments in your current relationship. Be as detailed as possible. Pretend someone else will be reading your text later; with your detailed description the person should see your situation as a film playing in front of their eyes. Ask yourself the following questions at each of those moments:

▼   What image or what picture best describes this situation?
▼   What kind of feeling does this situation give you? Give yourself a mark on a scale from 0 (= completely unhappy) to 100 (= supreme happiness).
▼   Where do you feel it?

What does this say about yourself? How would you finish the sentence "I am…"? Now put these moments on a graph. On the (horizontal) x-axis mark the age you were when the situation occurred, on the y-axis indicate how nice this situation was for you. Place a symbol for your most beautiful moments (for example) and a symbol for your biggest successes (for example a + sign). What kind of feeling does this diagram give you?

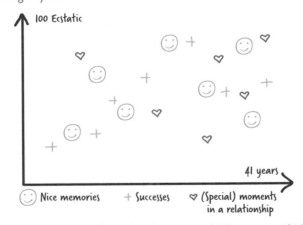

This exercise can be very difficult, but keep trying! Allow yourself 10 minutes per day to do this exercise. And keep in mind that the process is more important than the result.

Influence yourself

Feeling good is also determined by your genes. Compare it to predisposition for weight gain: some people were blessed with a slender body and don't need to work at it, while others merely have to look at ice cream and their scales tip. Although the exact share between *nature and nurture* will always remain a subject of discussion, it is a fact that there is a strong genetic basis in terms of happiness. In addition, a small part of it is also determined by your living conditions. You can imagine that it is less obvious to be happy in a war zone than in a rich, Western country. However, apart from our genes and our living conditions, there is still about 40% that we *can* influence by our daily thoughts and behaviours. So you do have the ability to consciously influence your feeling of happiness. It only takes discipline and self-control. It is therefore wise to choose the things that best fit your goal, means and way of life. This will greatly increase your chance of success.

EXERCISE
What makes you happy?

Make a list of five simple things that make you happy. Circle the three most important ones. Every day, try to do one simple thing that makes you happy.

1/ _____
2/ _____
3/ _____
4/ _____
5/ _____

Sonja Lyubomirsky, an American psychologist and author of the bestseller *The How of Happiness*, describes the most important characteristics of happy people:

○ They devote a large part of their time to their family and friends, cherish their relationships and enjoy them.
○ They do not find it hard to express their gratitude for everything they have.
○ They are often the first ones to offer colleagues or passers-by a helping hand.
○ They are optimistic about their future.
○ They enjoy the pleasures of life and try to live in the now.
○ They perform a weekly physical activity, sometimes even daily.
○ They are seriously devoted to their life goals and ambitions.

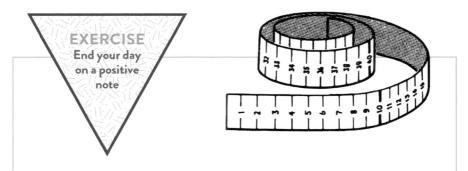

EXERCISE
End your day on a positive note

The following questions are a nice way to end your day as a summary to expanding your resilience.

▼ Did you do something fun today? If so, what exactly did you do?
▼ Did you do something good for your body? If so, what exactly did you do?
▼ Have you spent a moment alone? If so, what exactly did you do?
▼ Did you do something for someone else? If so, what exactly did you do?
▼ What is your good intention for tomorrow?

But he who is happy, can also suffer from stress. The difference lies in the reaction. Happy people bend like reeds and bounce back after the storm has settled. They don't fight the stress, but add the stress to their tool kit to learn from it. *Reculer pour mieux sauter*, as the French say it so nicely. Take a step back in order to jump forward. Or, as mentioned in many mindfulness books: you cannot stop the waves, but you can learn to surf. Feeling good is therefore above all a way of thinking, how we see ourselves and the world around us and how we approach it.

TIP / GO OUT FOR LUNCH

Just put everything aside, enjoy the food, talk with your colleagues. Know that if you skip lunch, your day will be less productive. You won't gain any time at all by skipping your lunch. If possible, go out to lunch once a week with someone who has nothing to do with work. Meet up with friends or acquaintances. You'll have something to look forward to: your lunch appointment. And let this be a good shield against stress and burn-out.

One of the ways to achieve growth is to accept that stress is part of your life. Life in balance is a myth. The truth is that we are always off balance to some extent. In this context, Machteld Huber speaks of **heterostasis**, the ability to adapt and control your own life. Change is everywhere, but you determine how to deal with that change. There are a few conditions however:

- ○ You take control of the reins.
- ○ You have a clear goal in mind.
- ○ You learn from your mistakes and failures.

EXERCISE
Everything
okay?

Every week, take some time to reflect on how you feel about yourself. These five short questions can help:

1/ Is everything OK?
2/ Experience any physical complaints?
3/ Have you had enough time to catch a breath?
4/ Do (did) you have enough time for yourself?
5/ Are you working on achieving your goals?

Each one of these questions can lead to the change that is necessary in order to reverse the negative effects of stress.

When you are in control of your life, when you have a clear goal and you are willing to learn from your mistakes and failures it is easier to throw your ballast overboard and choose your real goals, both private and at work.

Unfortunately, this is easier said than done. It requires exercise and daring to fail, it is a process of trial-and-error. It is, of course, important that you can fall in a safe environment and get back up again. Especially if you are in a phase in which stress is affecting you, you are not supposed to fall on purpose, just 'for practice'.

EXERCISE
Schedule your 'white' time

Set up a weekly schedule. Highlight the hours you work in blue, highlight your commute in red, time you spend doing house work in green and the hours you sleep in black. How many 'white' hours are left? How will you use these? Do this for every day of the week. How many white hours per week are there? There are 52 weeks in a year, of which an average of 48 have a normal time format. Multiply by 48 in order to obtain the total number of white hours per year (not including holiday periods). This is the time you can use for yourself. Spend it wisely.

Are you surprised by the little amount of 'white time' left? Then take a look at how you can extend this time. Are there are tasks you can delegate? Is working from home an option? Are there things that make you unhappy? Can you outsource these? Can you redefine the roles in your family so that everything is more equal?

Your action plan

Of course, changing yourself does not happen from one day to the next. It takes lots of practice and time. Having a good action plan is therefore crucial. When putting together an action plan, you can try to set as many concrete points in advance as possible. What do you want to work at? When do you want to work at it? Whom and what resources do you need? This goal-oriented approach provides a sense of control and manageability. For most people it is convenient, and in some cases, it is even necessary to steer a process this way.

EXERCISE
The tape measure
in you

Take a tape measure and see it as your life up to your current age. Highlight when you took on a job with responsibility, for example, as a leader in your youth group.

Now ask yourself the following questions:
- ▼ When did you feel at your best in this function?
- ▼ In what context were you working back then?
- ▼ What were your most important responsibilities?
- ▼ In general, how did you feel during this time?
- ▼ Do some of the answers above give you certain insights? For example, with regard to the context in which you function best or the responsibilities that give you the most satisfaction/result?
- ▼ Can you translate these insights into your current work context?
- ▼ What do you need in order to do so?
- ▼ How do you check whether you implemented these insights properly, or in other words whether you are on the right track?

There is just not one-size-fits-all solution. For some, a targeted approach can have a very stifling and crippling effect. In such case, it doesn't hurt to define your action plan and the efforts you will be making, less tightly. That way you add in time to adjust things along the way, as needed. Whichever approach you choose, a good goal oriented approach is based on your own responsibility and gives you the confidence, energy and flexibility needed to successfully complete a growth process and to sustainably expand your resilience.

Accept that growth and expanding resilience is a learning process that takes time. The big pit so many of us dig for ourselves is not giving it enough time. Therefore purposefully plan about ten minutes per day and an extra fifteen minutes per week. Use those fifteen minutes to evaluate your actions. What works for you in that moment or this situation and what doesn't? Also write down what works and impose discipline on yourself to persevere. But be kind to yourself. This is about the process, not the result.

The proof of the pudding is in the eating. It is therefore really crucial just to get started! The tips and exercises in this book will help you on your way. They all have a scientifically proven benefit, although you will notice that some exercises are easier for you than others. That is normal.

At the back of this book you will find some space to write down your own action plan. Keep it simple, short and engaging. Be realistic. Better one well-executed intervention than ten half-executed ones. Experiment. Does it not work? Then try to see what can be done differently.

TIP / TIPS FOR A GOOD ACTION PLAN

○ Assume that you need about ten minutes per day for yourself, every day of the week.

○ Make it a ritual, a fixed time of the day, so that it becomes a routine.

○ That moment is yours. It means you cannot be disturbed. So turn off all distractors, especially your smartphone.

○ Try to formulate your objectives as clearly as possible.

○ Convince yourself that your goals are important and achievable.

○ Record your progress on a weekly basis. Find out what works for you and what doesn't. And be proud of what you have already achieved.

○ Also schedule some time on a monthly basis to evaluate yourself.

○ After each month, indicate whether you would give yourself a sufficient or insufficient mark, for example. In case of an insufficient mark, check why that month didn't go as well. Often this will not be easy. Seek professional help if you keep stacking up failing marks or if you have the feeling you are not making any progress.

○ But maybe the most important tip is to be honest with yourself. You might be able to fool others, but not yourself.

Summary

○ If our stress system and our cockpit are properly aligned, we speak of resilience.
○ In order to expand resilience we must be focused on growth: focus on how to move forward.
○ Do not start at random, but set up an action plan for your interventions.
○ Use the exercises and tips from this chapter and keep in mind that the process is more important than the result.
○ Focus primarily on positive emotions.
○ Be aware that you always have a choice.

What will you remember from this chapter?

_____

_____

_____

_____

New insights:

_____

_____

_____

_____

How will you set out to do this?

_____

_____

_____

_____

3/ Be kind to yourself

Disadvantages of being a perfectionist

Striving for perfection is highly regarded in our society. Achieving high goals allegedly leads to great satisfaction. And it also helps you forward, for example in your career. But there is a fine line between realistic and unrealistic goals. Moreover, if you combine unrealistic goals with a very high level of self-criticism, you end up on treacherous terrain. Instead of becoming happy, you become stressed. You are afraid to make mistakes and nothing is ever good enough. Not achieving your goal is perceived as a failure. The least amount of critique is ill-received and your sense of self-worth decreases.

> **TIP / DON'T GIVE THE FULL ONE HUNDRED PERCENT**
>
> We were always taught to 'do our best', hence this tip may seem a bit odd, but still: try not to do your best. Remain at eighty percent of your capacity, both physical and mental capacity. That's how you keep a reserve and protect yourself from exhaustion.

TEST / 14 SINGS OF PERFECTIONISM*

The first step in guiding perfectionism in the right direction is to recognize it in yourself. The following test can help you on your way.

1. You often think of a mistake you made.
2. You are (very) competitive and can't stand it when you don't perform as well as others.
3. You either want to do things right or not at all.
4. You expect perfection from others and you often feel irritated because things and people around you do not meet this expectation.
5. You don't ask for help as this could be seen as an imperfection or weakness.
6. You persevere with a task long after others have given up.
7. You often feel overwhelmed with tasks because you always try to achieve a lot.
8. There never seems to be enough time to finish what you started.
9. You see mistakes in others and correct them when they do something wrong.
10. You are very much aware of the requirements and expectations of others.
11. You are embarrassed when you make a mistake in the presence of others.
12. You spend a lot of energy in keeping your life in order. You spend a lot of time making lists, planning, cleaning, repairing and less time on being creative and just letting yourself go.
13. You rarely stop to enjoy the success you achieved. You rarely feel proud that you have achieved something. You prefer getting on with the next item on the list that's waiting for you.
14. You noticed the error in the title of this list. *

Do you recognize yourself in some, a few or all of these signs? Then you may be (too) demanding on yourself. In our society, striving for excellence is generally regarded as an admirable mindset. Moreover, it helps us move forward in life. However, if this mindset takes on extreme forms, it can turn into maladaptive perfectionism.

EXERCISE
How workable is
your work?

What aspects of your work do you like? Of course not everything about your job is perfect, but surely there are some positives about it too. Take some time to reflect on this question. And it also helps tremendously if the working conditions are good as well. What are "good" working conditions? Shouldn't that apply to every job? Perhaps, but, in my book, good working conditions:

▼ do **not cause excessive stress**: How often are you exhausted and off-balance after a day's work? How much overtime do you work?
▼ offer **sufficient learning opportunities**: When was the last time you learned something new? When was the last time you received any feedback?
▼ are **motivating**: What is it about your job that makes you happy to start your workday?
▼ allow for a **good balance between work and private life**: Do you have plenty of time to have a rich private life?

Check how this is in your situation.

People with maladaptive perfectionism often set unrealistically high goals for themselves and are too critical of themselves. In addition to a lot of stress, this also causes them to have a lower self-esteem, less self-confidence and more shame. They start worrying about the 'mistakes' they have made and live in constant fear that the result will be disappointing. If you cannot live up to your unrealistic expectations, you will start seeing yourself as a failure, which leads to an even lower self-esteem. In addition, if mistakes are unacceptable, you are probably very sensitive to feedback as well.

TIP / SCHEDULE SOS-MOMENTS

Are you looking for space, time and a place to implement your changes? Schedule SOS moments. Keep them open and use them as a cushion for unexpected events or just to relax. Constant pressure and tension will just increase your level of stress!

And when perfectionists do reach their goal after all, they won't spend much time basking in the moment. Instead, they immediately move on to the next (unrealistic) task. This causes a lot of continuous stress, especially for some (maladaptive) perfectionists. It's therefore important to learn to recognize when your striving for excellence has morphed into striving for absolute perfection.

TIP / TIPS FOR PERFECTIONISTS

○ Be aware that you are demanding. In what areas of your life do you set the bar too high for yourself? It is not hard to figure that out. When do you not feel well? This may be an indication that your expectations are too high. Analyse the situations in this sense and make a list of the pros and cons of your high expectations.

- Test your expectations with the people around you. They will often give you meaningful feedback. It will help you balance your expectations better. Discuss with each task/job how everyone keeps track whether everything goes according to plan. Be specific about it. What type of behaviour do they expect? What results do they expect? Check whether these are realistic, given your current schedule. (Extra tip: if possible, schedule ten percent extra time for each task).
- Remember that to err is human. It is important not to try to desperately hide errors. Just be honest about it. Nobody is perfect.
- Differentiate between tasks that matter and tasks that aren't as important. And only give one hundred percent for tasks that really matter.

Demanding, perfectionism or high standards?

My perfectionist clients often ask me: "When is someone considered a maladaptive perfectionist and when not?" If I then confront them with their behaviour, they often respond scornfully: "What do you mean, isn't that normal?" Well, no, that isn't normal. At the most, it shows how distorted a perfectionist's standards sometimes are. Sometimes just stepping outside your own frame of reference helps. The following exercise will show you just how different we all are.

EXERCISE
Seeing the world through a different lens

Instruct everyone in your team or family to take a picture of a particular object or a particular situation. This is superfast thanks to smartphones nowadays. Then make a presentation with the pictures. How many different angles do you get? Not everyone sees the world through your lens. Each one of us does something different with a particular item. And one is not necessarily better or worse than the other. Some jobs require more precision than others. We expect a pilot or a heart surgeon to perform his or her work with the utmost accuracy. It is therefore 'normal' for people in these occupational groups to want to do things the right way, but slipping into pure perfectionism can be counterproductive.

In order to learn how to deal with negative beliefs, it is first and foremost important to be aware of erroneous ideas and their consequences. Here too, awareness through self-understanding is the first important step. The following exercise can help you with this. Think back to situations that gave you a bad feeling. Bad feelings or anxiety are often a good indicator of a need to dig deeper.

EXERCISE
Debunking negative beliefs

Check which (high) expectations and demands you set for yourself in that situation, and determine what pros and cons were associated with it.

You could also ask someone in your environment to see how high you set the bar for others. Then see which thoughts, insecurities or concerns form the base for these (high) demands. A few examples of irrational thoughts:

- ▼ 'There is a solution to every conflict and each conversation should always end in consensus.'
- ▼ 'I must make people happy.'
- ▼ 'Everything that happens in the department must be handled to the full satisfaction of the patient.'
- ▼ 'I must always show understanding.'
- ▼ 'I (or a doctor or nurse) should always be loved and respected by patients.'
- ▼ 'My colleagues should always love working with me.'

If you list these self-sabotaging thoughts, then also consider how you can reformulate these thoughts into a positive goal/positive thought.

Self-sabotaging thoughts	Self-supporting thoughts
There is a solution to every conflict and each conversation should always end in consensus	It's ok if people don't agree with me. I stand behind my opinion, choices, points of view…

Try to further concretise these self-supporting thoughts.

List all situations in which you had such a self-supporting thought. In the examples above, we are talking about situations where it was okay if others did not agree with your vision. How do you experience these situations? What did you do or say at that moment? Could you also use this method in current or future situations? How do you want to check and see whether the steps you are taking are heading in the right direction?

List all reasons why the self-sabotaging thoughts could not be true.
What positive feelings do you get when you debunk your negative belief?

The annoying thing about irrational thoughts is that we continue to have them without questioning them. We find it odd to tell ourselves "I always do everything right", but have no issue with the thought "I always do everything wrong.". Moreover, irrational thoughts invoke much more tension than positive thoughts, therefore imposing unnecessary pressure onto yourself. Therefore, dare to doubt yourself.

TIP / FIND YOUR INNER-GODZILLA!

Protecting yourself from irrational thoughts is not easy, precisely because they are provided by our auto-pilot. Everyone has them from time to time. I, for instance, will go into over-protection mode when I get the feeling I'm not good enough. My life as a scholar does not make it any easier for me: you are often rejected and brought down, and there is still the mentality of 'every man for himself' in the academic world. That is not my strongest point. So if I get the feeling that I'm not good enough, I go into defence mode. That is when my Godzilla appears, as I call it. Throughout the years I have become better at allowing my Godzilla to be an integral part of who I am; I no longer hide him, but I use him as a signal that in some area I am not being appreciated enough. I try to embrace it by seeing it as something we can learn from. And believe me: the one time it works better than the next, and that is not a big deal at all!

Does your Godzilla pop up from time to time as well? A handy tip is to behave like an OEC (see p. 88). But beware: choose your battles. You really do not need to always convince everyone all the time. So before letting your Godzilla out, think about this first: is it urgent and important for me to make a mark here? If yes: go for it! If not: write down why you would like to react, so that Godzilla does get some attention. Allow yourself some time each month to lay out your Godzilla notes and evaluate them. What are you missing when you read this? How can you solve this? During your next moment of self-evaluation, check to see how well you're doing.

Perfectionism in itself is not the problem here, but maladaptive perfectionism is. It leads to hardness towards yourself and constantly 'mulling things over' in your head (see also chapter XX). You no longer allow mistakes: "Failing is not an option!" However, failing is a part of life. When you stumble, you come to a standstill for a moment, giving you the opportunity to reflect on what did not go well.

TIP / GO GREEN

Green appears to be the colour that encourages creativity. One of the most important characteristics of green is that it automatically attracts attention without effort. This phenomenon is also referred to as 'soft fascination'. During the experience of 'soft fascination', worry, pain and stress fade into the background.

Failing is all a part of moving ahead! At least for some of us. There are others who don't seem to learn from their mistakes. In that respect, I am a fan of the research done by American professor and expert on motivation, Carol Dweck. She states that you can classify people on a continuum: from those people who are convinced that success is entirely based on their innate ability to those who are convinced that success is based on hard work, learning, training, and tenacity. The latter have a 'growth mentality', according to Dweck.

Here I let the words 'not yet' be my guide: **"I am not/don't/can't yet...."** This 'not yet' indicates you are in a learning process. These two powerful words also invite you to look back at the efforts you have made to date in order to reach your predetermined goal. In addition, they are also a strong antidote against worrying.

Worrying can have a crippling effect. A good way to deal with this is to schedule some targeted worry time.

▼ Set aside twenty minutes in your planner daily. During those twenty minutes, write down what is occupying you at *that* moment/what you are thinking about at *that* moment.

▼ Do this every day, all week long. At the end of the week read everything again and try to summarize the problems. Ask yourself with each problem why it is a problem, whether you can do something about it and if you can't, who can help you:

What is the problem?	Why is it a problem?	Can I do something about it?	If not, who can help me?

Now determine the order in which you want to tackle the problems. Give it a number. It is possible that something that is not as important, but easy to solve, receives priority. That's OK.

▼ Don't try to tackle all the problems at the same time, just do one at a time. Do keep to a pre-established timetable, so you don't drag your feet on certain things.

The power of self-compassion

Maladaptive perfectionism and harshness towards yourself mean that you will be living life too cautiously in order to avoid all pain in your life. This is how you remain in a constant, never-changing status quo. Your prefrontal areas are being extinguished due to lack of use. The solution to this is simple: other people. We must look for empathy and warmth. So ask for feedback or help to get you past the threshold. Look for role models in your organisation and get together every now and then. Ask them how they deal with failure and what they learn from it. And above all, be kind to yourself.

EXERCISE
Go for a walk!

▼ Walking has a beneficial effect. Label each inhalation and exhalation: '1... out ..., 2... in..., 3... out...' and so on.
▼ Walking and focusing on nature is one way to bring mildness into difficult situations. While walking, name everything you see: grass, tree, fence, apple...

This fits in seamlessly with the effect of mindfulness and self-compassion. One of the founders of the concept of self-compassion is psychologist Kristin Neff, also a practising Buddhist. Self-compassion means that you do not change how you view yourself when you are having a hard time, when have failed, or when there is something about yourself you don't like. Instead of ignoring your suffering, tell yourself: "I am having a hard time with this. How can I best comfort myself and take care of myself in this difficult moment?" Instead of ruthlessly judging yourself and criticising yourself for various shortcomings, self-compassion means that you are kind and understanding towards your mistakes and faults. You could, of course, try to change in order to become happier and healthier, but you do that because you care about yourself, not because you find yourself worthless and unacceptable.

> **TIP / GET A PET**
>
> Pets, such as dogs or cats, ensure you feel less stressed and happier. Or get an aquarium: dream away while looking at the fascinating colours of fish.

It is important here that you accept and respect your humanity. Things do not always go the way you want them to go. You will encounter frustration, loss; you will make mistakes; you will run into your own limits; you will not meet your own ideals. This is a reality we all share with each other. Open up your heart to this reality instead of fighting against it, and you will be able to feel compassion for yourself and your fellow human beings. A high degree of self-compassion will increase your motivation to deal with personal weaknesses and previous failures and ensure that they do not occur again.

As defined by Neff, self-compassion consists of three dimensions: self-kindness (vs. self-judgement), shared humanity (vs. isolation), and mindfulness (vs. over-identification). Let's take a closer look at these three dimensions.

TIP / SELF-KINDNESS IN DIFFICULT SITUATIONS

A few items to reflect on when things aren't going as well:

- What would a sweet, caring friend tell you in this situation?
- What might be a constructive way to do it better next time?
- Think of someone you love. Has your love for that person suddenly disappeared when that person has made a mistake or has had a bad day? No, right? So this shouldn't apply to you either.
- Be kind to your body: touch yourself, take a nice bath or shower, pamper yourself, especially if you're having a hard time!
- Nobody expects you to be perfect.
- How can you learn something if you never make mistakes?
- You do not necessarily have to bring order in the chaos of your work. (I am weighing my words carefully here, as for some this certainly couldn't hurt). In any case, it is more important to remember those things that are important to you. A clean desk is not necessarily a part of it.

Self-kindness

Self-compassion means that you are warm and understanding towards yourself when you suffer or if you feel you are failing yourself, instead of ignoring your feelings or drowning yourself in self-criticism. People with self-compassion know that imperfection, failure, and experiencing problems in life are inevitable. That is why they are kind to themselves when they experience something unpleasant, instead of becoming angry that life does not always go they wanted it to. People cannot always have or be everything they want. If you deny this reality or fight against it, your stress, frustration, and self-criticism will just increase. However, if you accept this reality with kindness, you will experience more emotional balance.

TIP / ACT LIKE AN OEC

Act like an OEC as much as possible when your alarm goes off:
- ○ Open
- ○ Empathetic
- ○ Curious

Imagine: you are attending a meeting and you feel personally attacked due to a comment or criticism. Instead of thinking how you will defend yourself, you could also try to examine the comment. Ask yourself why you've responded this way. Ask for more information if you need it.

Recently I was in a meeting where I launched a new idea. I had not quite completed my explanation and I was already being peppered with critical questions. My reaction: *'Thank you for your questions. I find myself making all kinds of assumptions about why you're asking all these questions. I was not quite finished with my presentation. I understand that this is a new idea and that I don't have everything fully fleshed out yet. I'm certainly grateful that today we can brainstorm together about this new idea. But I do need to maintain a certain structure, so I suggest that I first finish my presentation. I will then be glad to hear all comments. I suggest we pool all remarks and see how we can clarify and/or solve these remarks together.'* Instead of defending myself, I created space for myself and my presentation. The response from my colleague was: *'Oh yes, Elke, I think it's a great idea, I'm already thinking along with you on how we could improve it. Great idea to structure this. Sorry for the interruption.'*

I'm convinced that this mindset will help you to be resilient in a world full of change that requires us to adapt continually, as we already saw in chapter 2.

Common humanity
Frustrated that things are not as you want them to be often goes hand in hand with an irrational, but persistent sense of isolation, as if you are the only one who is having a hard time or making mistakes.

TIP / LOOK FOR A CONFIDANT

Find someone you can trust and with whom you can regularly discuss your situation and behaviour in an honest way.

All people suffer from time to time. A feeling of common humanity means that you can look at yourself as being mortal, vulnerable, and imperfect. Self-compassion means recognizing that suffering and imperfections are a part of the human experience we all share. These are things that we all experience and are not unique to you.

TIP / COMMON HUMANITY IN DIFFICULT SITUATIONS

○ Think of other people who make similar mistakes, have similar flaws and experience similar adversity. They are everywhere, you are not alone!

○ Others mean well. Not everyone has negative intentions.

○ What you are going through is part of being human: we are all vulnerable, we all have flaws, we make mistakes, we experience painful things, we are rejected.

○ How can this situation teach you more about people and give you more compassion for others?

○ Take responsibility for your behaviour and your choices, but keep in mind that your behaviour is affected by the behaviour of others: nothing happens in a vacuum.

○ Do something nice for someone else. Don't sit around and wait until someone else does something nice for you. You'll feel better right away!

○ It often seems as if you are the only one who doesn't belong or who isn't good enough, while others enjoy each other's company, can handle anything they do, are never insecure or lonely, etc. In reality, we all sometimes feel like we don't count. That is exactly what connects us with each other.

Mindfulness

Self-compassion means that you approach negative emotions in a balanced way, so that they are neither suppressed nor exaggerated. This balance is created by relating your personal feelings to the feelings of others, helping you to see the situation in a broader perspective. Someone with self-compassion is prepared to view their own negative feelings and thoughts with openness and clarity; focusing on them without losing themselves in it. Mindfulness is a non-judgemental, reflective state of awareness in which you look at your own thoughts and feelings as they are, without suppressing or changing them. If you ignore your pain, you cannot have compassion. At the same time, mindfulness requires you not to identify with your feelings and thoughts and not to let them swallow you.

TIP / MINDFULNESS IN DIFFICULT SITUATIONS

- ◯ Strengthen your mindfulness with (zen) meditation or yoga.
- ◯ Take a raisin (or a piece of apple). Don't just eat it like you always do, but give it some extra thought. Take a good look at its shape, colour and texture. Smell it. Hold it against your lips before putting it in your mouth. Focus on just this raisin in this moment. Put it in your mouth, but don't start chewing yet. Feel how it feels. Then, slowly start chewing. It does not really matter how you do this, what is important is that you are focused on the here and now. As you look at the raisin - carefully, without wanting to change it - that is how you can look at your own feelings and thoughts.
- ◯ At a difficult moment: take a deep breath and feel what you feel, exactly how it is, without ignoring your pain or exaggerating it. Consider what you are feeling: it is what it is. Open your heart to what you feel, without resistance, with calmness and clarity. Accept this moment completely as it is.
- ◯ Feel your bodily sensations exactly how they are (for example tension in your abdomen, a lump in your throat), without getting lost in the story behind it.

- Don't be a drama queen (or king). This does not mean you should suppress your suffering, but you shouldn't make it worse than it is either. Do you tend to lean towards the role of victim? Then take a look at yourself and ask yourself what its function is.
- Keep in mind that feelings come and go. Even difficult feelings will pass. And you don't coincide with them: you are not your feelings, you have them.
- Don't take it all so personally!

When people have self-pity, they tend to drown in their own misery and forget that others could be having similar problems. They forget that they are connected to others and they have a feeling they are the only ones who are having misfortune. Self-pity puts the emphasis on egocentric feelings of isolation. It means that you will soon start exaggerating your misery. People with self-pity let themselves be carried away by their misery and personal drama. They are not able to take a step back and look at the situation from a broader angle. They feel victimised.

Step 1 Think of a situation that completely upset you, for example: This could be: "My husband never listens to me when it comes to his health."

Step 2 Now turn this statement around, in three ways: Turn "My husband never listens to me when it comes to his health" into...
1 "I never listen to myself when it comes to my health."

Can you come up with three situations for which this statement is true? Are these the same situations that apply to your husband?
2 "I never listen to my husband when it comes to his health."
Find at least three examples that support this argument.
3 "My husband does listen to me when it comes to his health."
Find at least three examples that support this argument.

Step 3 What insights does this provide? As long as you keep thinking that the solution is 'out there' or as long as you keep thinking that something or someone else is responsible for your suffering, you will be stuck in the role of victim and you will be exploited by your stress brain. It is high time you find take charge of the ship!

In the case of self-compassion on the other hand, you see the relationship between your own experiences and those of others, so you don't feel isolated. By taking the perspective of someone who looks at you with compassion, you create a mental space in which you can place your experiences in a broader perspective and be able to relativize. Moreover, it also sets off self-satisfaction, because it ensures that you want to grow and develop yourself. At the same time, self-compassion also offers a sense of safety, necessary to see yourself as you really are, with all your weaknesses, but without condemning yourself.

EXERCISE
Handling
rejection

No one likes to be rejected. Feeling safe in a group is considered one of our basic needs. Fortunately, there are ways to better handle a 'no'.

▼ **Ask questions when you are rejected.** The magic words are 'what makes...'. Often this will bring to light the underlying reason for the rejection and it gives the rejected person a chance to solve the problem in a different way.

▼ **Retreat (without fleeing).** By not giving up after a rejection, instead making a less demanding request, chances are you will still get a 'yes' for an answer.

▼ **Work together and do not start an argument.** Everyone is entitled to their opinion. Look at the goal: do you have that in common? Then try to work together to find a solution.

▼ **Engage in dialogue, but don't give up.** If you are about to give up, take a step back and see if you can submit your request to someone else, in a different environment, or subject to other terms.

Summary

- Perfectionism itself is not wrong, it does however become a problem when you don't allow errors for yourself.
- Maladaptive perfectionism makes it harder to deal with stress.
- Perfectionists can help themselves by increasing self-kindness.
- Insights from mindfulness, such as self-compassion, can help here.

What will you remember from this chapter?

_____

_____

_____

_____

_____

_____

_____

_____

New insights:

_____

_____

_____

_____

_____

_____

_____

_____

How will you set out to do this?

4/ Prevention is better than cure

Prevention is better than having to find a cure, especially when it comes to chronic stress and burn-out. People who are confronted with burn-out sometimes need months or even years to regain their stress resistance. In this chapter I would therefore like to focus on the importance of a good lifestyle and proactive coping, so that you don't end up being burned-out.

Advantages of being a proactive coper

Proactive coping means that you recognize, acknowledge and then anticipate undesirable situations and deterioration to prevent future problems. After all, life consists of a succession of things that don't go as well as you planned. Be aware of that and try to prepare for it. We notice that whomever scores well in this regard, generally suffers less stress-related problems. However, someone who has less developed coping skills, will go through the stress continuum faster. In other words: he who appears at the start well prepared, is better equipped to deal with the obstacles that will appear on his path no matter what. The harder you are on yourself, the more difficult it gets, as seen earlier in connection with maladaptive perfectionism and fear of failure.

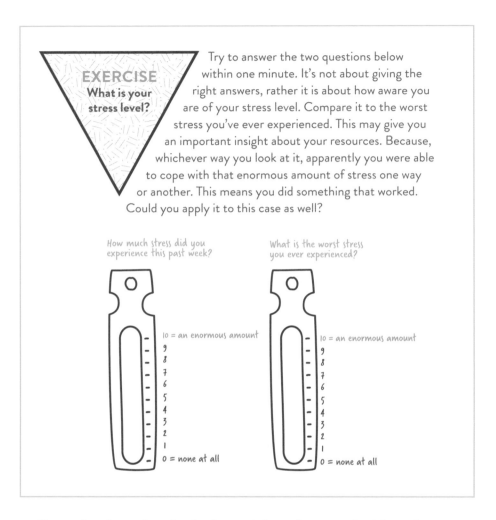

EXERCISE
What is your
stress level?

Try to answer the two questions below within one minute. It's not about giving the right answers, rather it is about how aware you are of your stress level. Compare it to the worst stress you've ever experienced. This may give you an important insight about your resources. Because, whichever way you look at it, apparently you were able to cope with that enormous amount of stress one way or another. This means you did something that worked. Could you apply it to this case as well?

How much stress did you experience this past week?

What is the worst stress you ever experienced?

10 = an enormous amount
9
8
7
6
5
4
3
2
1
0 = none at all

10 = an enormous amount
9
8
7
6
5
4
3
2
1
0 = none at all

Remember the explanation in chapter 1 about the neurophysiology of stress? Research shows that chronic stress causes the ability to control life proactively to disappear. That's because chronic stress affects the operation of your prefrontal cortex. When the prefrontal cortex no longer functions properly, you will have problems with inhibition, initiative, your frame of reference, and your perception of pain.

Inhibition

Someone whose inhibition is hindered can no longer differentiate: everything becomes equally important. You will see people wandering the corridors in overworked departments. If you limit these people's movements by placing them in a chair, the prefrontal cortex's functioning will deteriorate, which is exactly the opposite of what you want to achieve. Moving stimulates the prefrontal cortex, which means better inhibition. You need stimulation, not inaction! That's why it's so important to schedule sufficient physical exercise, even if it does not seem possible with your busy schedule.

Initiative

The initiative to move is very fragile. People whose prefrontal cortex no longer functions properly are no longer able to show initiative. They stall; their creativity is at a standstill... Everything goes back onto auto-pilot and every challenge is met with the same solution.

> **TIP / FIND A HOBBY**
>
> Find a hobby. It doesn't matter which one. Find something that suits you, that gives you satisfaction, and from which you can learn something. Or start a collection. People who collect things seem to be happier than people who don't have a collection.

Your own frame of reference

If your prefrontal cortex is affected by an accident or a stroke, it may be that your personal history has been erased. You come, as it were, out of nowhere. This also means that you no longer remember how you used to be able to successfully solve a problem. Continuous stress causes your prefrontal cortex to function less, and therefore you will handle similar problems with remembered patterns.

Perception of pain

You do still experience pain, but you can no longer label it as such. Pain can therefore still be a reason for anxiety/agitation, but you no longer know its cause.

TIP / HOW DO YOU RECOGNIZE AN OVER-ACTIVE STRESS BRAIN?

An over-active stress brain has the following characteristics:
- ○ Difficulty suppressing sudden ideas: taking immediate action without considering whether it is the right moment.
- ○ Displaying socially desirable behaviour: all is well.
- ○ Being distracted by every internal and external stimulus and having the feeling that nothing ever comes of it because the focus is constantly shifting from one thing to the other.
- ○ Becoming very rigid on a behavioural level: always reacting the same way to every challenge, question, wish...

The golden circle

Your prefrontal cortex functions better in a challenging environment. Asking why is very important in this respect: Why do you do what you do? Simon Sinek created a simple but very powerful model for this: the golden circle. There are three questions in that circle: What do you do? How do you do it? Why do you do it?

Sinek states that everyone knows *what* they are doing. Some may indicate *how* they do it, but only few also pay attention to the *why*, with all the associated consequences. Instead, we rush from task to task, but can no longer see the broader picture. No wonder we are at risk of being collectively burnt out. We are too preoccupied with the what, where, and when, and therefore fail to get to the why. However, if we want to remain inspired by our work, we need to find out what it is exactly that drives us.

The answer to this question gives direction and perspective and allows us to take the wheel of our career ourselves.

The art, therefore, is to be able to read the golden circle from the inside out: start with why and the rest will follow.

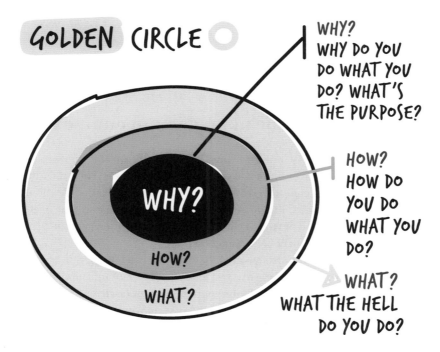

WHY?
WHY DO YOU DO WHAT YOU DO? WHAT'S THE PURPOSE?

HOW? HOW DO YOU DO WHAT YOU DO?

WHAT? WHAT THE HELL DO YOU DO?

Figure 4 / The golden circle. The art is to read from the inside out: start with why and the rest will follow.

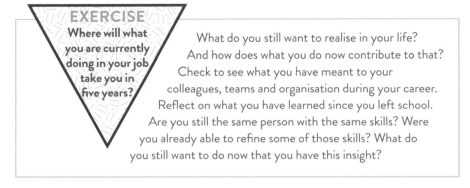

EXERCISE
Where will what
you are currently
doing in your job
take you in
five years?

What do you still want to realise in your life?
And how does what you do now contribute to that?
Check to see what you have meant to your
colleagues, teams and organisation during your career.
Reflect on what you have learned since you left school.
Are you still the same person with the same skills? Were
you already able to refine some of those skills? What do
you still want to do now that you have this insight?

The myth of time management courses

As mentioned in chapter 1, our prefrontal cortex is able to lead from above, independently from the influence of each emerging impulse. The prefrontal cortex keeps the goal in mind and every choice is weighed against this goal. Whatever does not contribute to meeting that goal is eliminated. The executive function is created partly for this reason, giving us a sense of the big picture which allows us to achieve our goals.

Your prefrontal cortex also ensures that you can track time. But when stress blocks your prefrontal cortex, you lose your sense of time and you remain stuck in the moment without a sense of past, present, or future. Time suddenly seems to go very quickly, giving you the impression you are increasingly getting less done, resulting in even more stress.

TIP / TALK ABOUT YOUR WORK

Have a positive conversation about work with a colleague and discuss:
- ○ a moment in the recent period that provided satisfaction;
- ○ recent progress in something that is important to you;
- ○ a conversation you had that you were satisfied with;
- ○ something you tried recently and which succeeded.

"Everything is possible with the right planning." That's what time management courses have been telling us for years, but it is a lie. Time management leads to fragmentation: we try to tick off as many tasks as fast as possible off our endless to-do list, and lose sight of the bigger picture. It's not about organising your time down to the second so you are able to do as much as possible. Do what you're supposed to do and do it well: that's what it's all about. In other words, we need attention management instead of time management: focus and maintain your concentration without being distracted by other things.

The following exercise can be done individually or in a group.

- ▼ What would you like to finish in the next 2 to 3 hours?
- ▼ Work for 45 minutes, without distractions.
- ▼ Take a break and evaluate.
- ▼ Find out how others could help you.
- ▼ Continue working for 45 minutes, without distractions.
- ▼ Take a break and evaluate.
- ▼ Find out how others could help you.
- ▼ Repeat if necessary and as possible.

A healthy mind in a healthy body

First and foremost, I am a psychologist, not a dietician, sports coach, or mother-in-law, but nevertheless do allow me to step outside my field of expertise for a moment and draw some attention to a healthy lifestyle. If you smoke like a chimney, barely sleep, eat an unhealthy diet, and are a couch potato, then I can tell you right now that the exercises in this book won't help you much.

I could have started the book with this chapter, because it is extremely important and it should be obvious. But every day I take a look around and see that this is not the case.

Allow time to recover

As you can see in figure 5, recovery goes with ups and downs. Keep track of how many 'good' days you've had and read your 'wow' folder on days where things aren't going as well (see p. 40). Pick a buddy you can call on those days when things aren't going as well and listen to their counsel, even if you don't feel like it. It will keep you active, even when things aren't going as well.

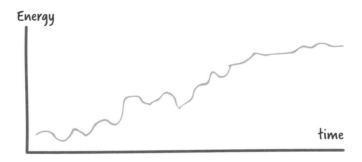

Figure 5 / Recovery always goes in ups and downs. Off days are part of it.

Eat healthy!

As the saying goes, you are what you eat. If this is true, I don't have a good feeling about who we are. In general we eat way too much junk. We engross ourselves in sugar, fat, and meat and many of us suffer from a chronic lack of fruit and vegetables. It is beyond the scope of this book to go into detail here. Be guided by one of the many healthy cookbooks found in bookstores.

Move!

Globally, people move less and less. This is alarming, as physical activity is very important for body and mind. By exercising you reduce the risk of high blood pressure, heart and circulatory diseases and type 2 diabetes. This, in turn, ensures you are less likely to suffer from dementia.

- ▼ Check the weather forecast on the internet for the next seven days
- ▼ Write down the forecast and think of what you want to do in your spare time.
- ▼ Make sure you have some passive and active leisure activities. Exercising is in our nature.

EXERCISE
Check the weather

Our brain will therefore function better when we exercise more. Especially our so-called 'executive functions' benefit from sports. These executive functions are responsible for planning, controlling impulses and self-regulation. We need all these functions in order to function independently. So go see someone instead of calling or messaging him or her. Take the bike instead of taking the car or bus. Make sure you don't gain too much weight; exercising is more pleasant when you're not overweight. Are you taking care of someone who is not able to do all of this on their own? Try to help him or her stay physically active as well.

Exercise and activation are very important in self-care. As mentioned earlier, exercise ensures that your hippocampus keeps feeling well and that it continues to exercise its inhibitory function on your stress system. In addition, exercise also releases recovery hormones. And it helps with a smoother removal of waste from your body. In short, exercising should be at the top of your list. And because a lot of exercise has disappeared from our lives, it is necessary to compensate.

Look in the mirror and ask yourself whether you exercise enough. Many people think they do, but grossly overestimate themselves. When I ask who keeps to the standard of sufficient exercise during lectures, I see most people happily raising their hands. But when I then tell them that exercising twice a week isn't enough if you sit the rest of the week, I notice people are surprised. And if I then indicate that you need to exercise for thirty minutes straight, without a break, for better brain function, usually the rest of the hands are lowered quickly. And when I finally indicate that you should move every 45 minutes, at best one solitary hand is left.

TIP / TIPS FOR MORE PHYSICAL ACTIVITY

A few tips that hardly take any extra effort:
- Take the stairs instead of the lift.
- Go for a daily walk (for example, during your lunch break).
- Go grocery shopping on foot or ride your bicycle, walk the kids to school, bike to work...
- If you do take the car, park it farther away on purpose, so that you still need to walk.
- Do some gardening or clean the house.
- Stop emailing your colleagues. Meet up with them and discuss business while walking.

Even when you are recovering from burn-out, exercise is important from day one; we then speak of activation. Go for a walk or bicycle ride at least once a day. It doesn't need to be far, as long as you do it. Find (possibly together with your therapist) a sport that fits within the limits of your current physical capabilities. There is no need to become an intensive endurance athlete all of a sudden. The most important is the focus on moderate exercise. As a rule of thumb, you can keep in mind that while exercising you must still be able to talk with your sparring partner (or if you are alone: to hum a song).

EXERCISE
Play!

Playing is not something just for kids! Playing relaxes us and teaches us without realizing it. Play half an hour per day. Choose games you enjoyed playing before you were twelve years old. Sing, move and do rhythmic exercises for optimal sensory integration. Guess objects with your eyes closed to stimulate your sense of touch and remove defragmentation. Or roll a tennis ball under your foot to return to the here and now.

Sleep!

Finally, just a few words on sleep. We spend about a third of our lives sleeping. It is not yet entirely clear why. It is certain though that we need that sleep. During sleep, the brain fuels up on new energy in the form of glycogen. This glucose storage diminishes during the day.

If you don't sleep enough, you will notice it right away. Sleep deprivation affects the way our brain functions, resulting in bad or poor performance during the day. Hence there are a multitude of problems that result from sleep deprivation. The main ones are memory and concentration issues and a delayed reaction speed. But also your physical preparedness and your emotions are negatively impacted due to lack of sleep.

The importance of sleep and the seriousness of the problems caused by sleep deprivation are still heavily underestimated. Research shows that in about 30 percent of traffic accidents, sleep deprivation was a crucial factor. Unfortunately, our contemporary attitude towards time is not to our advantage. We now sleep about an hour less every night than we did forty years ago. That is a lot of missed sleep!

Nowadays we go to bed with the idea that the day was far too short. We can no longer relax, and are running from evening meetings to parties. And if we do sit down, we are busy with our online friends on social media.

Combined with the sometimes ridiculously high demands we impose on ourselves, it is the ideal excuse to chip away bit-by-bit at our sleep time. Apparently, as a society, we are not yet convinced of the importance of a good night's rest. People everywhere insist (and rightfully so) on the importance of exercise and healthy food, but sleep always seems to be let off the hook.

The minimum amount of sleep needed in order to properly function varies from person to person. Not everyone needs eight hours of sleep per night. Moreover, the amount of hours says nothing about the quality of your sleep. When your alarm goes off in the middle of a dream or when you are in the deepest sleep phase, you will still feel lousy when getting up. It is therefore extremely important to base your need for sleep on how you feel during the day.

Unfortunately, we live in a society that almost considers sleep to be sinful. Effort is rewarded, relaxation isn't. This way of life leads to high brain activity so your brain is still running at top capacity at the moment you should be sleeping and even in the middle of the night.

TIP / TIPS FOR A GOOD NIGHT'S SLEEP

○ Go to bed when you feel sleepy.
○ Tired ≠ sleepy! When you are sleepy, you are way past the tired-stage.
○ Exercise regularly, but allow for enough time (two to three hours) between exercising and the moment you go to bed.
○ Don't lie in bed tossing and turning for hours. If you can't sleep, get up and go to a different room. That's how you prevent the brain from linking the bedroom to being awake.
○ Keep to a regular sleep-wake schedule so your internal clock doesn't need to adjust itself every time.

○ Avoid naps after 3 pm or that last for more than 20 minutes.

○ Be careful with alcohol, it disrupts deep sleep.

○ Don't make a habit of thinking about what happened that day or what will happen the next day when lying in bed.

○ Don't worry right away if for some reason (such as stress) you are not able to sleep well for a few days. Your 'sleep debt' will rise and at a certain point you will start sleeping better on your own again. Also, don't go to bed too early and avoid sleeping in late.

Summary

○ Proactive coping means you are able to recognize and acknowledge undesirable situations and retrogression and be able to anticipate this to prevent future problems.

○ Listen to your environment.

○ Create routines of what's good for you.

○ If you master these skills, you will be better armed against stress.

○ A healthy lifestyle helps prevent stress symptoms and burn-out.

○ Eat healthy, exercise, sleep!

What will you remember from this chapter?

New insights:

_____
_____
_____
_____
_____
_____
_____
_____

How will you set out to do this?

_____
_____
_____
_____
_____
_____
_____
_____
_____

'Be a beacon,
not a lifebuoy!
A beacon will lead
you onto the right
path, a lifebuoy
will drag you down
when overloaded.'

— Elke Van Hoof

Your own action plan

Here you can list all insights this book has given you. What exercises
worked for you? When can you work on your resilience? Are there any other
insights you would like to add to this book? In short, the following pages are
for you to fill in! Enjoy your stress, and don't forget: you are not alone!
For more tips go to www.huisvoorveerkracht.be.

Thank you

Expertise is not something you build on your own. I would therefore like to thank everyone who contributed to this expertise. It is still an honour.

Thank you, Lannoo. Katrien, Wim and all the others...

If you want to learn more or take it a step further:

- www.elkevanhoof.com
- www.huisvoorveerkracht.be
- www.reboarding.be

Bibliography

Bohlmeijer, E., Bolier, L., Westerhof, G. & Walburg, J.A. (2013). *Handboek positieve psychologie*. Amsterdam: Uitgeverij Boom.

Diener, E. (1984). Subjective Well Being. *Psychological Bulletin, 95*, pp. 542-575.

Diener, E. (1994). Measuring Subjective Well Being: Progress and opportunities. *Social Indicators Research, 28*, pp. 35-89.

Diener, E. & Diener, C. (1996). Most people are happy. *Psychological Science, 7*(3), pp. 181-4.

Diener, E., Emmons, R.A., Larsen, R.J. & Griffin, S. (1985). The Satisfaction with Life Scale. *Journal of Personality Assessment, 49*, pp. 71-75.

Jefferson, A., Himali, J., Beiser, A., Au, R., Masaro, J., Seshadri, S., Gona, P. et al. (2010). Cardiac index is associated with brain aging: the Framingham heart study. *Circulation, 122*(7), pp. 690-697.

Kemeney, M. (2003). The psychobiology of stress. *Current directions in psychological science, 12*(4), pp. 124-129.

Klaver, M. (2015). *Zakendoen met emoties. Limbische verklaring en cognitieve emotieve behandeling bij SOLK*. Amsterdam: Uitgeverij SWP.

Laurent, H.K., Laurent, S.M. & Granger, D.A. (2014). Salivary nerve growth factor response to stress related to resilience. *Physiology & Behavior, 129*, pp. 130-134.

Lyons, D.M., Parker, K.J. & Schatzberg, A. (2010). Animal models of early life stress: implications of understanding resilience. *Developmental psychobiology, 52*(7), pp. 616-624.

Neff, K.D. (2003). Development and validation of a scale to measure self-compassion. *Self and Identity, 2*, pp. 223-250.

Piefer, C., Engeser, S. (red.) (2012). *Psychophysiological correlates of flow-experience. Advances in flow research*, pp. 139-164. New York: Springer.

Ryff, C.D. & Singer, B. (1998). The contours of positive human health. *Psychological inquiry,* 9(1), pp. 1-28.

Seery, M. (2013). The biological model of change and threat. Using the heart to measure the mind. *Social and personality psychology compass,* 7(9), pp. 637-653.

Su, R., Tay, L. & Diener, E. (2014). The development and validation of Comprehensive Inventory of Thriving (CIT) and Brief Inventory of Thriving (BIT). *Applied Psychology: Health and Well-Being,* 6(3), pp. 251-279.

Taylor, S. (2006). Tend and befriend; biobehavioral bases of affiliation under stress. *Current directions in psychological science,* 15(6), pp. 273-277.

Van den Berg, A.E. & Van Winsum-Westra, M. (2006). Ontwerpen met groen voor gezondheid; richtlijnen voor de toepassing van groen, *Healing environments,* 15, Alterra.

Van der Kolk, B. (2014). *The Body Keeps the Score. Brain, Mind and Body in the Healing of Trauma.* New York: Penguin Random House.

Other books by Elke Van Hoof:

○ Burn-out in health care. What you should know (co-authors: Gorik Kaesemans, Lode Godderis, Erik Franck)
○ The Chief Happiness Officer. Roadmap to a strategic policy for occupational well-being.
○ First aid for high sensitivity
○ High sensitivity. What you should know

www.lannoo.com
Register on our website and we will send you a newsletter on a regular basis
with information about new books and containing interesting exclusive offers.

© Uitgeverij Lannoo nv, Tielt, 2017 and Elke Van Hoof
Editors: Wim Degrave
Translation: Textcase, Deventer, The Netherlands
Design: Nele Reyniers/Studio Lannoo
Author's photo: Marco Mertens
Illustrations: Nanoe Carremans
D/2018/45/202 – ISBN 978 94 014 4804 8 – NUR 770

No part of this publication may be reproduced and/or published by means of
printing, photocopying, microfilm, or by any means without the prior written
permission of the publisher.